CISTERCIAN FATHERS SERIES : NUMBER SIX

WILLIAM OF ST THIERRY

Volume Two

EXPOSITION ON
THE SONG OF SONGS

CISTERCIAN FATHERS SERIES

Board of Editors

CISTERCIAN FATHERS SERIES: NUMBER SIX

THE WORKS OF
WILLIAM OF ST THIERRY

Volume Two

Exposition on
the Song of Songs

translated by
Mother Columba Hart OSB

introduction by
J. M. Déchanet OSB

SHANNON · IRELAND
1970

The translation here presented is based on the critical Latin text prepared by J. M. Déchanet OSB and published in the *Sources Chrétiennes* by Les Éditions du Cerf.

Copyright © Cistercian Publications Inc., 1969

Ecclesiastical permission to publish this book was received from Bernard Flanagan, Bishop of Worcester, December 25, 1968.

SBN 7165 1006 5

Irish University Press Shannon Ireland
DUBLIN   CORK   BELFAST   LONDON   NEW YORK
T M MacGlinchey publisher
Robert Hogg printer

Printed in the Republic of Ireland by
Cahill & Co. Limited, Parkgate Printing Works, Dublin

CONTENTS

SECOND SONG

INTRODUCTION

When William of St Thierry entered Signy in 1135,[1] he brought along a literary background that was already significant: three treatises—*On Contemplating God,*[2] *The Nature and Dignity of Love,*[3] *The Sacrament of the Altar,* written about 1128.[4] In addition, there was a collection of *Meditations,*[5] his colloquies with God, and a

1. The excellent pages that Dom Jacques Hourlier has written on William of St Thierry, his environment and his spiritual itinerary, in the Introduction to *The Works of William of St Thierry,* vol. 1 (Cistercian Fathers Series 3) make it unnecessary to present William to the readers of Cistercian Fathers Series.

2. In vol. 1 of *The Works of William of St Thierry* (trans. Sr Penelope CSMV). This translation is made from the edition of Dom J. Hourlier (*Sources Chrétiennes,* No. 61 [Paris:Cerf, 1959]) which is based on a manuscript of Reuil, presently at Paris, Mazarine 776, which seems to come directly from the autograph.

3. *De Natura et Dignitate Amoris,* PL 184: 379–408—the twin treatise of the preceding. See J. M. Déchanet, *Oeuvres Choisies de Guillaume de Saint-Thierry* (Paris: Aubier, 1944), pp. 151–213, and M. M. Davy, *Deux Traités de l'Amour de Dieu* (Paris: Vrin, 1953); Cistercian Fathers Series 15.

4. *De Sacramento Altaris,* PL 180: 345–366. After the *Golden Letter,* the treatises *On Contemplating God* and *On the Nature of Love,* it is this treatise of William's that has been most often copied. But this little eucharistic summary, so representative of the theology of the twelfth century with the sort of *sic et non* approach found in it (see our study: "L'amitié d'Abélard et de Guillaume de Saint-Thierry" in the *Revue d'Histoire Ecclésiastique,* 1939, pp. 761–774), has not served its author's cause any more that the treatises which were attributed to St Bernard. A good thirty manuscripts can be counted of which only two or three bear William's name. The others are anonymous or under the patronym of St Anselm.

5. Also to be found in volume 1 of William's works in the present series.

good-sized file of notes on his reading. These he doubtless planned to put in order rather than further develop.

Though later rich in manuscripts of all kinds, Signy, newly established abbey that it was, offered very little to William's studious avidity. However, his classified notes were to give rise to a whole series of compilations: *Exposition on the Epistle to the Romans*,[6] *Excerpts from the Books of Saint Gregory on the Canticle of Canticles*,[7] *Commentary on the Canticle of Canticles Drawn from the Works of Saint Ambrose*,[8] *The Nature of the Body and the Soul*,[9] *Axioms of the Faith*[10] (composed after 1135 and before 1145). To his

---

6. *Expositio in epistolam ad Romanos*, PL 180: 547–694. Of this treatise there exists only one manuscript, part of which is in the author's own hand.

7. *Excerpta ex libris Sti Gregorii Papae super Cantica canticorum*, PL 180: 441–474. This work may have been compiled by William during his abbacy. It is significant that one of the rare sample manuscripts, perhaps the only one, comes from Saint Thierry of Rheims (today, Rheims 142, twelfth century, folios 67–85).

8. *Commentarius in Cant. Cant. e scriptis S. Ambrosii*, PL 15: 1947–2060. Referring to this compilation addressed to Dom Haymon, prior of Mont-Dieu (cf. his letter in *Scriptorium*, 8 [1954], pp. 259–261), William characterizes it as "a great and renowned work." Very lengthy—it covers 113 columns of Migne; celebrated—it has known some success; its oldest manuscript, the original or first edition, is Rheims 142, twelfth century, folios 1–60. But there exist other copies almost as ancient: Paris, B. N. lat. 2647, twelfth century, from Saint-Martin de Tournai, folios 37 ff.; Brussels, Royal Library, 19066, thirteenth century, from the Abbey of Parc de Louvain, folios 1–60; Paris, B. N. lat. 561, thirteenth century, folios 1–42.

9. *Domni Wilelmi* [corrected from Willelmi] *abbatis S. Theoderici "De Natura Corporis et Animae Libri Duo sub Nomine Theophili id est Deum Diligentis descripti."* This is the complete title of the work in original manuscript, Charleville 172, folio 113, transcribed at Signy in the twelfth century. This title is, however, posterior to the copy of the text, hence the mention of the abbacy which they liked to remember after William's death, even at Signy. The work figures in PL 180: 696–726; trans. Cistercian Fathers Series 24.

10. William mentions these to Prior Haymon, but they have not been found.

meditations he was to add others according to the aspirations or vicissitudes of his interior life.[11] From among these he was to make a selection to be placed at the disposition of beginners in the art of prayer.[12] He felt himself ready to augment his youthful treatises on the love of God by others more profound, because of his later reading and reflection; and he desired to review his favorite themes and to sound them to their depths. Above all, he wanted to make God the object of a constant and loving consideration, the hiddenness of which, made easier by his new state in life, was to be the measure of his devotion and fervor.[13] This he wanted to live even to the gift of self, to total adherence to the Divine. That is why, having become a simple monk once again and relieved from the obligation of writing or speaking on specified dates for the benefit of others, he dreamed—yet without excluding some possible reader or other— of working finally for himself, of realizing the projects of days gone by.

11. One was discovered among William's papers after his death. It was transcribed at the end of the twelfth century on two pages that had been left unfinished (folios 75v–76r) in what is now the Charleville collection 114. The monks of Saint-Thierry, also, had discovered a similar paper. It is the Prayer (*Oratio Domni Willelmi*) which figures in the Reuil manuscript, Paris Mazarine 776, and is found in translation in volume 1 of *The Works of William of St Thierry* in this Series. It is also worthy of note that Tissier inserted it after the *De Natura Amoris* in vol. IV of his *Bibliotheca Patrum Cisterciensium*, Bonnefontaine, 1662, pp. 58–59.

12. "I wrote," he was later to say in his Letter to Prior Haymon, "some meditations which are not entirely useless for forming the souls of novices in prayer" (*meditationes noviciis ad orandum formandis spiritibus non usquequaque inutiles*). It is this collection that the manuscript of Reuil (Paris, Mazarine 776) presents under the title of *Meditativae orationes: Incipiunt Meditativae Orationes Domni Willelmi, Abbatis Sti. Theodorici*, folio 1. The *Vita Antiqua* (Paris, B. N., lat. 11782, twelfth century, folios 340 and 341, published by Poncelot in *Mélanges G. Kurth*, vol. I, Liège, 1908, pp. 89–96) likewise says: "He composed a somewhat lengthy tract which is entitled *Meditations*" (*Composuit et tractatum non parvum cuius est epigramma Meditativae orationes*).

13. See how touching are his avowals in nos. 3 and 5 of the *Exposition*.

Conceived as early as his very first visits to Clairvaux,[14] the *Exposition* or *Commentary on the Song of Songs*, which he completed as far as the first verses of the third chapter, was to be the fruit of the intimate and restful happiness of long, carefree days.[15] Much too soon he would have to interrupt it in order to attend to Abelard.[16] Unfortunately for us, he would never be able to go back to it.

14. In his *Life of St Bernard* (XII, 59; PL 185: 259a–260a), William tells how, when sick, he was sent to Clairvaux by St Bernard who was himself suffering from the stomach pains that hardly ever left him. Immobilized in the monastery infirmary, the two friends entertained each other throughout the long days with "spirituality" (*tota die de spirituali physica animae conferabamus*). If we are to believe the little tract that seems to have been the direct result of this encounter (cf. Dom J. Hourlier, "Guillaume de Saint-Thierry et la *Brevis Commentatio in Cantica*" in *Analecta Sacri Ordinis Cisterciensis*, 12 [1956], pp. 105–114), William brought to the discussion especially his penetrating analysis of the different "states" of the interior life of which we shall speak further on. Bernard contributed something else: the art of "interweaving" the religious and mystical experience of a soul into the web of a piece of sacred writing, the Song of Songs. Assuredly, William knew the text and the diverse historical and allegorical interpretations to which it had given rise. He knew them so well that he had begged his friend "not to touch upon the mysteries hidden in the Holy Book, but only to draw from this last a purely moral interpretation," that is, an application to the spiritual life. But from the very first exchanges, he was keenly aware of the particularly bookish stamp of his own knowledge. Bernard showed him those things "which one knows only by experience," and William perceived what he lacked—what his love lacked—for an understanding of the colloquy between Bride and Bridegroom, or to be able himself to sing, as he was to do later on, the sacred canticle of love. Perhaps he had already begun the compilations of which we have already spoken (the extracts from Gregory and from Ambrose). It is certain that the encounter at Clairvaux gave rise in him to the project of a wholly personal commentary that would be the mirror of his interior life. This is but one more claim that St Bernard has on our gratitude.

15. "A fertile sloth" (*Pingue otium—Golden Letter*, no. 13), "delightful sloth" (*delicatum otium—Letter to Prior Haymon*)—so William characterizes the happy period of his first years at Signy after his resignation as abbot.

16. Here is how he explains himself in this regard in his *Letter to Prior Haymon* (no. 4): ". . . on the Song of Songs, up to: When I had little passed by them, I found him whom my soul loves. Then I wrote against Peter Abelard which prevented me from completing the aforesaid work, for I didn't think it right that I should be enjoying such a delightful leisure inside, while outside a drawn sword so to speak was ravaging the faithful."

After his *Dispute against Abelard*,[17] and the two books, *The Mirror of Faith* and *The Enigma of Faith*,[18] he was urged on by the love of souls and by gratitude to write *The Letter to the Carthusians of Mont-Dieu*.[19] Finally his affectionate admiration for the abbot of Clairvaux transformed him into the biographer, or rather the hagiographer of his saintly friend. Death claimed him soon after the opening chapters of the *Life of Saint Bernard*.[20]

In this collection, *The Exposition on the Song of Songs* stands out in sharp relief. It is no longer the mere plagiarism of the early treatises, nor an anthology of introductory materials. Here we cannot speak of something written to suit the occasion—an error to be combatted, some weakness in need of strengthening, a love to be stimulated. His originality stands out at first glance. A soliloquy in appearance, composed of devout, but disciplined utterances, it is the work par excellence of William's life. It is the secret of a soul—

17. The *Disputatio contra Petrum Abaelardum* (PL 180: 249–282) figures in the Charleville ms. 67 (twelfth century), originating from Signy, folios 72v–109r. The same codex provides us in folios 132r–138v with the original, *including author's corrections*, of another polemical work of William's, his letter to St Bernard in regard to the errors of William of Conches: *Dno. Bernardo abbati Claraevallis frater W. Claritatem Aeternae Visionis Dei* (cf. PL 180: 333–340).

18. Written "to console the brothers" of Signy who were troubled by the innovations of Abelard and others, the *Speculum Fidei* and the *Aenigma Fidei* were finally dedicated to Prior Haymon, as William tells us in his letter to the latter (nos. 2 and 3). The two "libelli" make up folios 46 to 109 of the Charleville ms. 114. The first has been published in the Bibliothèque de Spiritualité Médiévale: *Guillaume de Saint-Thierry. Le Miroir de la Foi* (Bruges: Beyaert, 1946) and will be published in English translation in vol. 3 of *The Works of William of St Thierry* (Cistercian Fathers Series 9).

19. This is the famous *Golden Letter* (*Epistola Aurea*), the critical edition of which is in preparation by *Sources Chrétiennes*. An English translation will appear in volume 4 of *The Works of William of St Thierry* (Cistercian Fathers Series, 12).

20. The original of the *Vita Bernardi* (PL 185: 225–268) might be the Troyes ms. in the Municipal Library 663 which came from Clairvaux. It has been translated into English by G. Webb and A. Walker: *Saint Bernard of Clairvaux* (Westminster, Maryland: Newman Press, 1960).

his own—within the limits of which he wishes to enclose himself.[21] It is the patient pursuit—too slow at times to suit the reader—of the author's plodding walks through his own interior and of the tender colloquies to which his steps give rise. But at the same time, it is also a cold and rational examination of the birth and development of the various episodes of this unheard-of adventure in which the human soul, captive to Christ and victor over sin, becomes the Spouse, and through him, with the help of the Holy Spirit, yields to spiritual union with God. In the atmosphere of this deliberately chosen coldness of judgment, ceaselessly overcome by warm effusions of gratitude, and amid the vivid descriptions of life in these states of soul in which the lucidity of the intelligence sees itself multiplied ten times over by the intuitions of love, the verses of that jewel of the Scriptures, the *Song of Songs,* are spread out before us. They are filled with a richness, at once human and divine, by the splendid images of Oriental poetry and the burning revelations of the Spirit that inspired them. The case in which William encloses this treasure sets off its unique beauty and we need not fear to compare it with any other which doctors or saints have prepared for it.

Upheld by the sacred text and abandoning himself to its soaring flight, the author rises to the highest summits to which his reflection and experience can lead him. It is a culminating point in William's spiritual writings and the most personal expression of himself. The works which came after it, addressed as they were to less advanced souls, are written in lower registers. But these, like his other works, can help us to a better understanding of the *Exposition* and, without anachronism, can serve to prepare the way to study it.[22]

---

21. "Restraining ourselves within ourselves and measuring ourselves by ourselves" (*Exposition*, no. 5).

22. In sketching William's spiritual itinerary, Dom J. Hourlier in his Introduction to the treatise *On Contemplating God* (*l.c.*) has shown clearly that certain of the works posterior to the *Exposition* brought the author to a fuller insight, of which we are the beneficiaries.

Principal Characteristics

William's *Exposition on the Song of Songs* is not an allegorical commentary but a moral one. At the very least it purposes to be so. From the start, we are informed of the author's objective: "We do not presume to treat," he says, "of those deeper mysteries the Song of Songs contains with regard to Christ and the Church . . . . We shall, as anyone may venture to do, touch lightly on a certain moral sense apropos of Bridegroom and Bride, Christ and the Christian soul."[23] To those who are more clever than he, and more adventurous too, he leaves the forest of allegory filled with shadows and mysterious hiding places[24] and furrowed by deep valleys filled with dense groves.[25]

Masters and doctors, Origen, St Ambrose, St Gregory, even St Bernard have explored this forest. Having followed in their footsteps (attention is called to his two allegorical commentaries composed of extracts from Gregory and Ambrose) William knows how difficult, how delicate, too, is the application of the general theme, the figures and the episodes of the most sublime of the sacred canticles to the mystery of the incarnation or to any other mystery. To undertake a typological or doctrinal explanation of so subtle and profound a text is to touch upon the very mystery of the Scriptures. Without a special mission and without special lights, no one can extract from the wax of the texts that exquisite honey hidden in its cells. But the moral interpretation—that intimate colloquy, mouth to mouth, as a friend talking to his friend, between

23. *Exposition*, no. 5.

24. It is St Bernard who speaks of the "shaded and deep forest of allegory" (Sermon Sixteen on the Song of Songs, no. 1).

25. "For two consecutive days," writes St Bernard, "we have travelled in this forest with glances at the tops of the trees and the peaks of the mountains, but the depth of the valleys and the density of the thickets are beyond our powers of penetration."—*ibid*.

the soul and Scripture, between the sacred text and the heart which lays itself wide open to receive its effusions—this moral sense wherein each discovers for himself norms, directives and, what is still better, the picture of his spiritual life, of the interior drama in which God and the soul are, by turns, the actors and the interpreters—everyone, says William, can aspire to it. And to make it easier for himself he proceeds to make a reservation: it is not *the* moral meaning of the *Song of Songs,* but *a* moral meaning, a certain meaning from among many others—*sensum moralem aliquem*—which, conformably with his scant talent, he will set forth in a few words.

Actually, William exceeds this program, and here and there he touches upon the sacred mystery of Christ and his Church. The drama of the Spouse and the soul takes place *in* the City of God, and the mystery of love with which the soul sees itself favored is but its own response to the mystical espousals of Christ and his Church. Free as it may otherwise strive to be, the twelfth-century moral interpretation of Scripture rests solidly upon dogma, and an author such as William is much too traditional to attempt to separate from the Christian mystery its mystical life and history.

In the wake of Origen and in imitation of St Bernard, he regards the *Song of Songs* as a nuptial poem, written after the manner of a drama, in dialogue style, and calling for characters and acting.[26] The love-plot which it unfolds is based upon a historical fact (the marriage of King Solomon with the daughter of Pharaoh).[27] But it might just as well be a fable, a piece of fiction, a parable. Little does it matter. In it William distinguishes four phases, four acts to be more exact, each reverting to an identical scenario but in a higher key than before. There is the enticement of love (*irritamen amoris*), the purifying trial (*actus purgatorius*), the repose (*accubitus*)—that is, the union of Bride and Bridegroom introduced by a nuptial song—and a special epithalamium, followed, three out of four times, by

26. *Exposition,* Prologue, no. 8.

27. *Exposition,* no. 9.

the plea: "stir not up nor make the beloved to awake till she please."[28]

With these explanations made, the road cleared—*itinere expedito*—the author hastens to begin the commentary on the *Song*.[29] However, at the last minute he changes his mind and, in a long dissertation, endeavors to link once more the development of the spiritual life as it appears in the various "songs" of the sacred text, with the famous theory which he is later to make the theme of his *Letter to the Brethren of Mont-Dieu*, that of the three "states"—the animal, the rational, the spiritual—of souls vowed to the perfect life and of the forms of prayer corresponding to each.[30] In another more concise and more technical form, these very weighty pages capture

---

28. *Exposition*, no. 7. William divides the canticle as follows: First Song: 1:1–2:7; Second Song: 2:8–3:5; Third Song: 3:6–8:4; Fourth Song: 8:5–14. For each Song he has written a Prelude (*Exordium*, cf. no. 145), in which he announces the unfolding of the action to follow. The terms mentioned above —*irritamen amoris, actus purgatorius*—are taken from the Prelude or *Exordium* of Song I, no. 29. In the very first song, William expatiates on the sentiments of the soul that "went forth from the storerooms in mature piety and sought anxiously for contemplation" (no. 114). He devotes four stanzas (nos. 30–61) to the "enticement of love." Stanzas 5 to 9 (nos. 62–113) describe the "purifying trial" of the Bride. Then comes the *epithalamium* or "nuptial song" properly so called: "The King brought me into the cellar of wine . . . stay me up with flowers," stanza 10 (nos. 114–131) and finally the "repose": "His left hand is under my head, and his right hand shall embrace me," stanza 11 (nos. 132–137). The "finale" (nos. 138–144) infringes a little on the matter belonging to Song II when it comments not only on verse 7: "I adjure you . . .," but also on the first words of verse 8: "The voice of my Beloved." At the Prelude of the Second Song is announced the scenario (no. 146) in terms somewhat different from those of the first: "hope hastens, desire becomes a crucifixion" (*spes festinans et crucians desiderium*, stanzas 1–3, nos. 147–166), "wisdom sets all in order" (*sapientia ordinans*), i.e., purification (stanza 4, nos. 167–168); "love speeds forward" (*amor currens*) in the *epithalamium* preceding the second "repose" (stanzas 5 and 6, nos. 179–203). The last act, complete union (*mutua conjunctio*), is lacking because the *Exposition* was interrupted.

29. *Exposition*, Prologue, no. 11.

30. *Exposition*, nos. 12–24.

the reasoning of the whole *Commentary*. We shall come back to this when we speak of the doctrine and its sources.

Its Doctrine

There is no better introduction to William's *Exposition on the Song of Songs* than his own *Mirror of Faith*.[31] One of the theses of this work—of supreme importance in several respects—is that, for man here below, there are two ways of reaching God: first of all by faith, and then by the love that is charity. Christian faith is a knowledge acquired by hearing. It is a perfect adhesion, positive and deliberate, to truths that have been taught, that are foreign to the intellect and that can be known only through divine revelation. Furthermore, unlike the vanities of this world, these truths are intended less to enrich the mind than to nourish and invigorate the soul, to permit it to taste God, to enjoy him even in this life. What is more, it is above both "science" and "wisdom": an intellectual knowledge, but one in which love already has a role to play, a role all the more pronounced in proportion as the believer is advanced, more caught up by the truths to which he gives his assent. It is undoubtedly understanding but it is also pleasure, experience, profound life.[32]

To understand it we must really grasp what faith offers us and also the manner in which we adhere to its object. William tells us:

> Created for eternity, equipped intellectually for God, and destined to enjoy him, our mind finds itself bound to divine and eternal realities by a certain affinity and to such a point that, even should it become stultified by vice, it would yet never lose its appetite for things invisible. Their knowledge is inherent to reason and so deeply rooted that the mind cannot escape from

31. As will be remembered, this was written two or three years later.
32. *Mirror of Faith*, chap. VII, "The Object Proper to Faith," PL 180: 385 ff.

the love of the good and the beautiful, nor escape from the desire for blessedness and immutability, except, however, when in its desire, its appetite for truth is deceived by the "appearance of truth" or its love of good beguiled by some mirage. All that is the work of creative grace in us. Indeed, there must be an intervention of illuminating grace for the soul to see perfectly what its appetite for truth already enables it to glimpse. In order for it to apprehend this good which is drawing it, God must enable the soul to grasp it.[33]

That is indeed the work of faith. By faith, we seize upon Truth, Goodness, Beauty, God himself—not, it is true, directly, but through the sacraments, the mysteries, which are the proper object of Christian faith. "More deeply embedded in us than any of those faculties which go to make up our interior man," God communicates himself to us only by means of "intermediaries" exterior to himself as well as to us.

The reason for this economy is to be found in our nature: as bodies and souls we are habituated to reach to truth in the domain of earthly things through the mediation of the senses. It is only fitting that the senses should not be excluded from our initiation into the divine life, that the whole man—and not just his spirit— should participate in the experience of the things of God. To this reason of fittingness is added another—that of necessity. We are sick. The sacraments are the remedies for the particular kind of sickness which is ours since the fall. After rebelling against God in the earthly paradise in a movement of pride, our spiritual faculties find themselves compelled to yield to the corporal appearances of the corporal sacraments and, in this act of humility, they rediscover the road to heaven.

Faith, which supposes the sacramental economy, purifies our hearts, merits truth for us. In Eden, God spoke directly to the father of humanity. Since the fall, he speaks to us through his mediating Word. And it is through him, God and man, through his life, his

33. *Ibid.*, 386bc.

B

birth, his passion, his death and his resurrection; it is through his words as they are reported to us in Scripture, that we are constrained to pass in order to find God once again. It is he himself, this Word of God, who is at once the source and the greatest of all the sacraments of faith.[34] "The man," cries William, "who finds his own image in the Lord who is our Mediator does not sin, as Job assures us. When indeed the mind gazes on Christ and when it thus represents to itself God in the form of a man, it in no way strays from the truth. By not separating God from man in the unique person of Christ, faith grasps God in man."[35]

First of all, therefore, one must believe in Christ, one must welcome Christ, the sovereign remedy for our inflating pride—Christ, the marvelous sacrament of our regeneration,[36] but also and above all, the revelation of the Father and, by his life as by his words, the supreme mirror of Truth, the image of the invisible God.[37]

This is the first degree—still very humble—of the faith: not to refuse in one's heart the grace to welcome truths coming from outside and channeled through Christ and his message.[38] The beginner, the average Christian, he whom William calls "the animal man," often remains at this first stage. Incapable of seizing upon what is of God, he sees only irrelevance both in the ensemble and in each of the truths which he accepts solely on the recommendation of divine authority. He does not sense, he does not "realize" the intimate correspondence of these "exterior" truths with the secret

34. *Ibid.*, 382ff.

35. *The Golden Letter*, no. 174. The same idea, illustrating the text of Job, is to be found in the tenth Meditation and in the *Exposition* itself, no. 17.

36. "(God-made-man) the supreme remedy for healing our tumor of pride; the greatest Sacrament for our redemption": (*Deus factus homo*) *ad sanandum superbiae nostrae tumorem summum medicamentum; ad redemptionem nostram altum Sacramentum*—*Mirror of Faith*, PL 180: 385a.

37. William insists on this fact, that "all the acts of the Word made flesh are just so many words addressed to us" (*ibid.*, 386d) and that all his acts, all his words, are one and the same revelation of God (*ibid.*, 396c).

38. *Ibid.*, 387a.

aspirations of the spirit of man. This will be the part of the "rational," the second degree of living faith.

At this level one binds oneself to the truths of faith by friendship. After accepting them, one contacts them. Then there is a sort of marriage within man, between these "acquired" truths and the "immanent" truths, those eternal realities to which the spirit of man finds itself linked, as we said above, by a certain affinity and whose existence and attraction he naturally perceives when he is fully rational and fully himself. By meditating upon the work of the Redeemer, he discovers in it the most beautiful, the most gripping, and the wisest illustration of this kindness, of this power which his reason sees in God. Reciprocally—like a mutual exchange—the kindness of God, his wisdom, his omnipotence, in so far as it is humanly possible to conceive them, seem to give to Christ and to his message their full signification.[39] Undoubtedly, faith remains faith: an enigmatic knowledge and in a mirror. But the revealed data become clear. Their unity, their beauty appear in a special light. Best of all, a delightful enjoyment accompanies this knowledge, a sort of experience of the mysterious realities which go to make up the object of faith.

This, then, is the third stage. The *science* which is born of faith and which addresses itself to the reasonable part of man, is changed into *wisdom,* takes hold of the heart, installs itself in the mind. Henceforth, one knows Christ no longer according to the flesh. It is in him, the Word of God, eternal and immutable, that one is held. More exactly, the gaze of enlightened faith—of loving faith—begins to grasp, in the one and unique person of the Mediator, both the divinity irradiating its majesty from the humanity it has assumed, and the humanity projecting on the deity the brilliance of its humility.[40]

Above all, to the understanding one has of him, is added that

39. *Ibid.,* 387ad.
40. *Ibid.,* 386cd.

which is sweeter and more efficacious—a pious sentiment of love, of a supra-human love that comes from above and which is pressed to make its own, in the fullest measure possible, the sentiments of Christ Jesus; in other words to "feel" towards God as Christ "felt," to know God as Christ knew the Father—in love and in the substantial love which is the Holy Spirit.

The last part of the *Mirror of Faith* describes the "mechanism" of this knowledge of love, proper to the spiritual man, to him who is moved by the Spirit and who, from clarity to clarity, is raised to the very summits of the contemplative life. For if the second stage of the life of faith is under the aegis and in the light of Christ, the third is entirely an operation of the Spirit.

"It is one thing," writes William, "to know God as a man knows his friend; it is another thing to know him as he knows himself. To know, in the ordinary meaning of the word, to know a man or a thing, is to bear away in one's memory the image of what has been conceived by means of sufficient vision. Thanks to this image or phantasm one can represent to oneself the thing or person, even though absent, and recognize it when encountered. With respect to God, this common knowledge is the knowledge of faith."[41] By faith, indeed, we know God thanks to the concept of him given us by the Person, the Life, the Words of the Christ-Mediator, the Image of the invisible God impregnated with his Substance.

By looking at, by listening to Christ, we have learned that God is a Father, a father full of tenderness, of mercy, especially of love for his children, the creatures bought back by the Blood of Christ. We have learned of the existence in God of a Son, eternally begotten by the Father, equal to the Father and, together with him, the principle in the Deity of a third Hypostasis—the Holy Spirit. Most especially, we have learned that God himself is love. All these *notions* are in our memory like so many images. We have only to

41. *Ibid.*, 392d.

evoke them and right away God reveals himself to us—a God which our reason left to itself would never have discovered. God reveals himself to us as a friend reveals himself to his intimate, under an aspect, beneath a form, which a stranger cannot grasp.

Special and intimate though this may be, this knowledge resulting from faith which allows us to see God as it were in thought, by ourselves, is nevertheless not the full knowledge to which we aspire and for which we are made. Our desire can be fulfilled only by that singular knowledge that issues from charity, which is proper to the life of heaven, and which allows us to contemplate God in that ardor of mutual love which causes him to live in us and causes even us to be transported in him.[42] Here below, this knowledge is but a rough outline and William has taken the trouble to describe its development as accomplished through the knowledge of faith.

The soul has two senses: an external sense for the perception of bodies and corporeal substances, and an internal sense for the perception of spiritual substances. This internal sense is the intellect. However, a nobler and stronger sense, a more refined intellect, is love— on condition that it be pure.[43] Indeed, the Creator is perceived by the creature by means of love, as if it were an organ of sense or a consciousness giving an insight into God.[44] To understand this, one must realize that all sensation supposes a certain transformation of the sentient being into the object sensed, a presence of the one to the other, a certain penetration of the one into the other. This is similarly true of all knowledge. Now love has the power to conform the one who loves into the image of the object loved, of transporting them one into the other, and to do this more efficaciously and more completely than can be done by the external

42. St Stephen is, for William, the type of those who are transported to God by a form of loving ecstasy; Mary Magdalen the type of those whom simple faith keeps at a distance (cf. *ibid.*, 390bc).

43. Quite properly does the *Exposition* include purification, the liberation of love. The theme is announced in the very first sentences, nos. 1–4.

44. *Mirror of Faith*, PL 180: 390d.

senses or by the intellect.[45] These latter do not transform the mind
of man into the sensible and intelligible nature—the condition *sine
qua non* of all sensation or intellection—until they have first assimilated the sensible and intelligible and have in some way drawn them
into the soul where the abstraction takes place which produces
the image or knowledge of the object.

Love behaves otherwise. Endowed with the singular power of
transporting itself into the beloved and then of dilating itself in
proportion to its object (contrary to the intellect which, ultimately,
is always constrained to trim its object to its own capacities) it
reaches out toward being as being in the concrete reality of its
essence and its indescribable existence. Like the senses or the intellect it effects the assimilation of the subject to the object, but the
union it realizes is much deeper than that resulting from an act of
sensation or intellection. Unquestionably, the one who loves is in
the beloved immeasurably more than the one who sees is in the
visible body, or than the one who reasons is in the truth he desires
to attain.

Above all, he is particularly in the beloved in a manner which is
more intimate, more lasting, and also more real, for love is not a
static or congealed thing. It tends to grow ceaselessly. It is not
unilateral, but ordinarily—always when it is a question of God and
the love of friendship—it supposes a reciprocity of affection and
sympathy. It is repose in the one loved, but a repose consisting of
participation and exchanges. For that matter, it is not an exaggeration to affirm that it establishes, between the subject and the object,
something more than a community of life: a community of being.

By transfusing the lover into the beloved, love establishes a
certain connaturalness between the one and the other, and so it is
that it is even able to obtain for the former a *sui generis* knowledge
of the latter. Undoubtedly this knowledge is supra-rational but,

45. "More in this strong, loving affection than in the bodily senses or in
the rational intellect" (*Plus in hoc valente amantis affectu quam vel sensu in
corporalibus vel in rationalibus intellectu—ibid.*, 391b).

although it is not composed of distinct ideas, of concepts and phantasms, it is, none the less, an understanding as real as it is delightful. It is only the intuition of love, or that love-knowledge of which William speaks constantly, following St Gregory and the whole Greek tradition, which can, in the final analysis, come near to the burning bush and penetrate into the otherwise inaccessible Holy of Holies of the sanctuary of the Deity.[46]

Indeed, the knowledge of love, when it is a question of God, presupposes the intervention of the Holy Spirit "by whom does he who loves, love that which should really be loved."[47] For William, the love of the perfect Christian, of the spiritual man, is in some way mingled with the substantial charity of God, and this because love, in the measure that it purifies itself and is transformed into charity, is informed, assumed, absorbed by the Holy Spirit. "The love of God is conceived in the soul by faith, begotten by hope, formed and vivified by charity. In fact, God's love or God-Love, the Holy Spirit, in penetrating into man's love, sets it apart for its own use, and God, by drawing his love out of man, unites to himself both the mind and the love of the latter."[48] "Our love, when God is concerned, is the Spirit who is given to us and by whom charity is diffused in our hearts."[49] So frequently does this theme appear in William's writings that it is commonplace, but it provides us with the final, theological and mystical reason for the privilege of love.

Love does not unite us to God, love does not transform us into God, love does not cause us to see God except in so far as it is pure,

---

46. The reader is referred to my study "Amor Ipse Intellectus Est" in *Revue du Moyen Age Latin,* 1 (1945), pp. 349–374, for the doctrine of love-knowledge in William of St Thierry, where this key position of our author, supported by texts, is reviewed in all its forms.

47. *Spiritus sanctus . . . de quo amat quicumque amat quod vere amandum est—Mirror of Faith,* PL 180: 391a.

48. *The Golden Letter,* no. 170.

49. *Expositio in Epist. ad Romanos,* PL 180: 593c.

in so far as it comes from God, in so far as it is divine and deiform.
Now this marvel is realized when the Spirit, uncreated subsistent
Love, divine Charity, flows into us, and informs our own love and
dilates it in some way to the measure of its object. Then our heart
is filled with an ineffable light. We are ready to "taste," to see
"how sweet the Lord is"; in short, to experience God in so far as
the Holy Spirit himself would have us do so.

Even now, inasmuch as it comes from us, inasmuch as it incar-
nates our appetite for the Good, the Beautiful and the True, love
can secure for us a certain knowledge of God owing to the instinc-
tive feeling that urges us to model ourselves upon the object of our
desires.[50] Vehement though it may be, however, our appetite is
powerless to confer upon us anything other than a faint likeness
and this is why the knowledge that comes from active love (or
affective love, which is the same thing) remains obscure and remote.
On the other hand, should the will which is tending resolutely
toward God—this is the love of desire—should this will be "seized"
by the Holy Spirit and should the loving soul be suddenly transformed completely, not into the divine nature but into some form
of supra-human and quasi divine beatitude;[51] if it should come to
know dilection, should be enflamed by charity, should attain to
unity of spirit—the supreme degree of passive love—then it will
be launched upon a truly ineffable experience. It will progress from
clarity to clarity, from likeness to likeness until it arrives at
mystical union where knowledge attains its greatest acuity through
a certain vision. It is then, writes William, that the soul finds itself
in some way seized in this embrace and in this kiss of the Father

---

50. *The Mirror of Faith*, PL 180: 391bc. This is St Augustine's point of view
in *De Trinitate*, XI, 1, 5.

51. . . . *cum Spiritus Sanctus voluntatem hominis sic sibi afficit ut Deum amans
anima, et amando sentiens, tota repente transmutetur, non quidem in naturam
divinitatis, sed tamen in quamdam supra humanam, citra divinam formam beati-
tudinis.*—*Mirror of Faith*, PL 180: 391d.

and the Son which is the Holy Spirit.[52] Possessing in herself, rather, possessed by him who is found to be the substantial knowledge of the Father and the Son in the bosom of the Trinity, how can she fail to participate in the knowledge that God has of himself? There is knowledge because there is possession, penetration, inhabitation of the one in the other. The soul is no longer alone before God, a distant, inaccessible God, as in the knowledge of faith. The soul is with God, the soul is in God. It is not she who transforms herself into the image and resemblance of the object of her desires; it is he himself who seizes, penetrates, transforms her by the mediation of love and by the all-powerful action of him who, in the bosom of the Deity, is Love, Charity: the Holy Spirit. The soul is no longer the friend of God; she is the spouse in all truth and it is as such that she participates in that mysterious knowledge that two spouses have of each other, with this difference: as one of the partners is God, the mutual possession is infinitely more intimate and, in consequence, the knowledge, too, is more intimate, more profound—to sum it all up, it is unique.

The *Mirror of Faith* brings us to the threshold of the *Exposition on the Song of Songs* because it is precisely the adventure of the soul-bride that this last describes for us. We leave the field of theory for that of experience. But we must not forget: this whole experience is based on Christian faith. Never would the soul have been admitted into the intimacy of the Beloved, into the "cellar of wine" of the sacred canticle, had it not first passed through the "store-rooms" of the divine King.

The Sources

This simple analysis, or rather this plagiarism of the arguments of the *Mirror of Faith,* dispenses us from giving a commentary on the doctrine of the *Exposition.* The reader has in his hand the thread

52. *Ibid.,* 394b, and, in another connection, *The Golden Letter,* no. 263.

of Ariadne which will permit him to follow William anywhere and, with him, to "hasten by the quickest way after the Bridegroom."[53] It is, however, necessary to consider the important problem of the sources.

Personal as the *Exposition* may be, the author, although "restraining himself within himself"[54] and wishing to appeal only to the experience of love, in a word, his own love, could not but remain faithful to this natural penchant which he has of thinking with the Bible and its first interpreters: the Fathers of the Church.

The Bible

Like the treatise *On Contemplating God,* the *Exposition* is a perfect model of biblical style.[55] A commentary on Scripture, it is Scripture that provides its warp and woof. The opening paragraphs, in which William's favorite biblical themes are closely knit together, are typical in this respect. On every page the express quotations are to be found, whether in support of an argument or as the beginning of a new development in the outline of the *Exposition.*[56] It is an important fact that the author does not permit himself to be distracted from his subject and one cannot but admire the naturalness and the appositeness of his scriptural insertions.

Particularly striking are his outbursts into series of biblical metaphors to which the images of the sacred canticle give rise. The "sun has altered my color" of chapter 1, verse 5, for example, calls for the "sun of justice" of Malachi 4:2, and the "glowing coal" of

53. *Exposition,* no. 11.

54. *Exposition,* no. 5.

55. Cf. Dom Hourlier's Introduction, *l.c.*

56. See the developments introduced (no. 33) by the citing of Jn 14:28: "I am going away and I will come back to you," in no. 128 by the quotation from Eph 5:29: "No man ever hates his own flesh," and in no. 131 by the citation from Heb 8:5: "See that you do according to the pattern that was shown you on the mountain."

Psalm 119:4.[57] The "cellar of wine" of 2:4 recalls the "inebriating chalice" of Psalm 22:5, the "new wine" of Matthew 26:29, the "wine springing forth virgins" of Zechariah 9:17, the "wine of sorrow" of Psalm 59:5, the "wine that gladdens the heart of man" of Psalm 103:15.[58]

The "wall" of 2:9 becomes the wall over which we must go in Psalm 17:30, the "thick clay" of Habakkuk 2:5, and the "wall of separation" of Ephesians 2:14.[59] Farther on, the "clefts in the rock" (Song 2:14) remind our author both of Christ who is the "rock" (1 Cor 10:4) and of the "word . . . more piercing than any two-edged sword" (Heb 4:12).[60] On the theme of the two hands (Song 2:6) a complete network of Pauline citations is introduced.[61] This poem of the Bible, the Song of Songs is enriched in the *Exposition* by a delicate biblical poetry in which there are no false notes.

Bernard, Ambrose and Gregory

No less certain is the influence of several chosen masters on the thought and style of our author. One thinks immediately of St Bernard who inspired the *Exposition,* and, among the ancients, of St Ambrose and St Gregory whose works were thumbed through by William in order to get all the passages relative to the sacred Canticle.[62] Actually, the commentary includes only one or two pages of "Gregorian" inspiration and the style as well as the form of the great Milanese doctor are missing.[63]

---

57. *Exposition,* no. 50.   58. *Exposition,* no. 119.   59. *Exposition,* no. 155.

60. *Exposition,* no. 164.   61. *Exposition,* no. 136.

62. See above, footnotes 7 and 8.

63. *Exposition,* no. 80. Attention is also called to nos. 51 and 150 in regard to two ideas of Gregorian inspiration. On the one hand, the "onus" of honors in the Church; on the other hand, the "leaps" of the Redeemer. We must not forget that William doubtless owes to St Gregory not only the fundamental theme of his *Exposition,* but the formula which served him to illustrate the theme of *Amor ipse notitia est* ("Love itself is knowledge"—*Hom. XXVII in Evang.*).

As for St Bernard, if he is in a sense the "father" of the *Exposition*, if he has sown the seed of a true masterpiece, as was said above,[64] it must nevertheless be realized that in its form and in its expression, this masterpiece owes him nothing.[65] There is nothing typically Bernardine in William's application of the pericopes of the sacred text to his own spiritual life and to the mystical life in general. Neither is there anything particularly Bernardine in the wording and demonstration of the general thesis of the work: the liberation, the sublimation of love in the passage—under the action of divine grace—from the carnal, animal state, which is that of the simple Christian, to the spiritual state which is that of the soul-spouse.

Origen

This thesis comes from Origen, one of the themes that our author received directly from the Master of Alexandria, whom he never ceased to plumb throughout his entire literary career.

Origen, as we know, separates the faithful into three distinct categories: the beginners or *psychics,* those who have progressed or *gnostics,* the perfect or *spiritual.* The first, still the captives of their passions, bent beneath the shameful yoke of a fallen nature, have only the light of naked faith to guide them on their way of purification in their struggle against the vices. The second class,

64. See above, footnote 14.

65. In any case, he owes nothing to the saintly abbot's *Sermons on the Song of Songs* given in the chapter room of Clairvaux at about the same period. It is quite true that, by comparing the texts one with the other, one can pick out several verbal similarities, and so speak of a reciprocal influence. See, for example, nos. 108 and 110. The close connection, from the standpoint of inspiration, serves only to bring out the differences, as is the case in regard to the treatises on love by the two authors, as has been so well shown by Dom J. Hourlier: "Saint Bernard et Guillaume de Saint-Thierry dans le *Liber de Amore*" in *Saint Bernard Théologien (Analecta Sacri Ordinis Cisterciencis,* IX, 1953), pp. 225–233.

purified by the practice of asceticism, have their steps lighted by the torches of a sound reason and of an intelligent mind in full possession of itself, possessing, besides faith, a clear and certain knowledge of the mysteries which constitute its object. The third class, finally, at the summit of perfection, moved by a spirit intimately united to the Spirit of God, experience in some way in the practice of love the ineffable realities which are the matter of faith.

Each of these categories, then, marks for Origen a stage along the way of perfection. In the measure that the animal soul in the human composite gives way to the reasonable soul, and it in its turn allows itself to be informed by the Spirit of God, the Christian passes from the darkness of a blind and simple faith to the ever brighter light of an experiential wisdom. By working to purify his life and to detach his soul from the carnal and the sensible, he raises himself from asceticism even to contemplation; from the faith that battles and grieves to the love that tastes and enjoys, but not without first passing through the gnosis or intellectual knowledge of revealed truths. Pure faith, intelligence, love or wisdom—these are, for Origen, the three milestones that stand out in the soul's itinerary toward God.[66]

We have encountered this schema, or at least some part of this schema, in the analysis of the *Mirror of Faith*. It is to be found again throughout the entire *Exposition* and even from its opening pages, in a form and in terms that betray its origin. A thorough investigation of all of William's works would prove that this is not a fortuitous conjuncture, pure coincidence, but is the indication of an influence as clear as it is profound. Nowhere has William taken

---

66. The analysis given here of the spiritual itinerary according to Origen is obviously schematic. The trilogy of faith-intelligence-wisdom is to be found in the *Contra Celsum*, PG 11: 1309c. A more diversified exposition, and one more abundant in references, can be found in the article by K. Rahner: "Les Débuts d'une Doctrine des Cinq Sens Spirituels chez Origène" in *Revue d'Ascétique et de Mystique*, 1932, pp. 113-145.

one of Origen's major themes, and all that goes with it, and made it his own without re-thinking it along his own lines. He has truly assimilated them.

He must have become acquainted with Origen quite early—through some intermediary at first (perhaps John Scotus Eriugena)—and later directly.[67] Shortly after his entrance into Signy we find him in possession of a great deal of the *Corpus origenense* because the scribes of this monastery copied, in successive order, the *Homilies of Adamatius*[68] on *Genesis, Exodus, Leviticus* (Vol. I of ms. 207 of the Municipal Library of Charleville), the *Homilies on Numbers* (Vol. II), *on the Books of Joshua, Judges, Kings, the Song of Songs, Isaiah, Jeremiah, Ezekiel* (Vol. III); the *Commentary on the Song of Songs,* the *Periarchon*—both in the translation of Rufinus—(Vol. IV), the second part of the *Commentary on Saint Matthew* (Vol. V), and finally the extensive *Commentary on the Epistle to the Romans* (Vol. VI).[69] From this last work William was to do considerable culling, even while at Signy.[70] But well before, at the time of his *Letter to Rupert,* for example, he had already adopted one or other of its propositions—in particular, the tendency of the Alexandrian author to base himself on the distinction of St Paul between the "animal" or "carnal" man and the "spiritual,"[71] or to

67. Origen is the only "Oriental" whom he does not fear to name among his sources, for example, in the *Exp. in Epist. ad Rom., Prologus;* PL 180: 547a. In regard to this, see the remarks of H. de Lubac, *Exégèse Médiévale, les Quatre Sens de l'Ecriture,* part I, vol. I (Paris: Aubier, 1959), p. 230.

68. On this other name of Origen, "the man of diamond," see H. de Lubac, *op. cit.,* pp. 243–244.

69. The *Commentary* is followed by the *Planctus Origenis* of which H. de Lubac speaks, *op. cit.,* pp. 273–274.

70. Some fifty quotations from Origen varying from ten lines to the equivalent of one or two columns of Migne have been identified. Cf. J. M. Déchanet, *Guillaume de Saint-Thierry, L'homme et son Oeuvre* (Bruges, 1942), pp. 47–48 and p. 207.

71. In his *Letter to Rupert,* William writes: "The Apostle says: 'That your spirit and soul and body might be preserved for the day of the Lord' (I Thess 5:23). According to this division, which it is possible to find in every

develop the trichotomy of *corpus, anima, spiritus* of the First
Epistle to the Thessalonians in an explanation of the spiritual life.[72]

Actually, it is in the *Exposition,* at a time when we are certain
that he had Origen's work in his hands and from which he was
doing considerable borrowing, that we see the essentials of the
Origenist thesis being incorporated into the spirituality of our
author, and assume a visage that is proper to William.

The Pauline trichotomy *corpus-anima-spiritus* is left behind, while
at the same time he abandons the epithets of *corporalis* (or *carnalis*)-
animalis-spiritualis to designate, instead, the three degrees, the three
stages, or the three aspects of the life of man headed for perfection.
Another, more adequate, formula is presented to William in the
course of his patient delving into the writings of the ancient

---

man, two lines are seen, which are opposed to each other: the spiritual and
the animal. Of these three, namely, the spirit, soul and body, if the last two
serve the first, it is a spiritual life; if the first two serve the last, it is an animal
life" (PL 180: 344ab). For Origen: "Indeed, the soul, before it is converted
and becomes one with the spirit, adheres to the body and thinks of material
things. It does not seem to be in a good state nor in a bad one, but seems, as
I have said, to be like an animal. However, it is better that, if it can be done,
it adhere to the spirit and become spiritual" (*De Principiis,* III, 4, 3: PG 11:
323b). "When the soul subjects itself to the pleasures of the flesh, it makes the
man carnal; but when it unites itself to the spirit, it makes the man to live in
the spirit and because of this, he is called a spiritual man" (*ibid., II*: 322ab).
"Frequently we find in Scripture that man is said to be spirit and body and
soul. The soul is in the middle. It can rest in the desires of the spirit or stoop
down to the lusts of the flesh. If it turns to the spirit, it will be one spirit with
it. It follows that if it turns to the flesh, it makes the man carnal; if to the
spirit, spiritual" (*In Epist. ad Rom.,* 1:18; PG 14: 866a).

72. The same tendency becomes clear in one of the very first of William's
treatises, *On the Nature and Dignity of Love.* In it, William gives us a primary
sketch of his doctrine on the spiritual senses for which he is so deeply indebted
to Origen, as we have noted above (see James Walsh, "Guillaume de Saint-
Thierry et les Sens Spirituels" in *Revue d'Ascétique et de Mystique,* 1959, pp.
27–42, particularly notes 30, 50 and 52). In comparing the different forms of
love to the five senses, William calls attention to the fact that certain senses
are more "corporal" (*corporaliores*), i.e. primarily the instruments of the body;
others are more "animal" (*animaliores*), i.e. more at the service of the soul;
others, finally, are more "spiritual" (*spiritualiores*), i.e. more at the service of

Fathers and the "masters" of his time[73] and he does not fail to insert it into the *Exposition on the Epistle to the Romans*. In it he speaks of three "forms of the doctrine of faith"—*rationalis, spiritualis, intellectualis*—of three ways of receiving and embracing revealed truth. The first is acceptance, pure and simple, on the part of human reason (hence its name: *rationalis*) of the "sacraments" and the "mysteries" of faith (along with their requirements at the practical level of ethics and morals) just as they stand out in the teaching of the Savior. The second is the studious meditation, and even the contemplation "in the spirit" (*spiritualis*) of these same sacraments of the faith. Finally, the third, which is proper to hearts that have been purified, that merit to see God, is in the experience of illuminated love. It is intelligence (hence its name: *intellectualis*), but an intelligence that comes from above and not from human reason, from God himself, in his own light.[74]

---

the spirit, that "high part of the soul" (*principale mentis*). Cf. PL 184: 391b–392d. Again, is not Origen's influence sensed at the end of the treatise (PL 184: 404bc) when William begins to speak of the two branches of philosophy (wisdom), the science of human things and the science of divine things, and of the three degrees of knowing: the ethical, the physical, the theological? Cf. K. Rahner, "Les Débuts d'une Doctrine des Cinq Sens Spirituels chez Origène" in *Revue d'Ascétique et de Mystique*, 1932, pp. 129–130.

73. William tells us that he based his *Commenatry* on the authority of the great doctors: Augustine, Ambrose, Origen and others, and also, "some of the masters of our own times" (*In Ep. ad Rom.*, PL 180: 547a), "who," he adds, "we are certain, have not gone beyond the limits laid down by our Fathers."

74. "Others have placed three forms in the doctrine of faith: rational, spiritual, intellectual. The rational is in sacraments and customs proportionate to those men about whom the Lord spoke in the parables announcing the kingdom of God. The spiritual is in sacred reading and meditations, and in the greater doctrines, proportionate to those of whom the Lord said, 'To you is given to know the mystery of the kingdom of God.' The intellectual is in the enlightened love which belongs to the clean of heart who merit to see God. The rational demands voluntary obedience and active perfection; the spiritual, sobriety and humble contemplation, the intellectual, peaceful and familiar experience of God. This understanding comes from above, it is not formed by reason, but it conforms reason to itself, not that it might

In other words, it is really Origen's idea of the three successively higher landings leading from the simple faith of the humble believer here below, the beginner, the carnal or animal man, to the sort of anticipation of the face-to-face vision which is the knowledge of the perfect, the spiritual man.[75] But this idea which forms the basis of his spirituality William presents in a new way by choosing his vocabulary both from the one and the other formula.

The Prologue of the *Exposition* tells of the "states of soul" proper to men of prayer and of three ways of prayer proper to these states: the "animal," the "rational," the "spiritual." *Animalis, spiritualis*— these terms are taken from St Paul and from the formula of Origen.[76] William, with his gift for utilizing his sources, has created for himself a method of his very own[77] and one which will result in the success of a work such as the *Golden Letter*. In this last writing, moreover, it will justify itself by a whole psychology,

---

subject it, but illuminate it when it consents."—*Expositio in Epist. ad Rom.*; PL 180: 609d–610a. This text comes after a citation from the *Commentary* of Origen on the Epistle to the Romans, VI, 3; PG 14: 1059, where he writes: "The form of doctrine is that which we see here through a mirror in an enigma; doctrine itself is to see face to face, or the form of doctrine brought to fullness and formed by the doctrine of justice." The fact that the text previously cited is introduced by the word "Others" shows that it is not Origen's (even though the idea be his). Where did William find it?

75. This idea has been developed, as we have seen, in the *Mirror of Faith*.

76. We do not deny, however, that he might have borrowed the whole trilogy directly from Origen. This, it would seem, is the opinion of A. de Ivanka. Cf. "Apex Mentis, Wanderung und Wandlung eines stoischen Terminus" in *Zeitschrift für katholische Theologie*, 72 (1950), pp. 151 and 164.

77. The *Brevis Commentatio in Cantica*, to which we referred before, provides us, in that part "where the presence of William is manifest" at the side of St Bernard (cf. J. Hourlier, *art. cit.*, pp. 108–109), with an almost identical formula in regard to divine love which has "three states" (*status*): *sensualis vel animalis, rationalis,* and *spiritualis vel intellectualis* (cf. PL 184: 408). Nevertheless, this formula inspired by William (as proved by the word *status* which figures in the *Exposition* and in the *Golden Letter*) is not "his very own formula." It has been compared to that of Alcher of Clairvaux who speaks of three "forces" of the soul: *animalis seu sensualis, rationalis* and *intellectualis; cf. De Spiritu et Anima*, PL 40: 808.

C

which is lacking in the *Exposition*, but which will manifest once
again the influence of Origen on the thinking of our author: *anima*
which dictates the behavior of the animal man; *anima* which
becomes, which must become, *animus*[78]—what is this if not the
ψυχή of the Doctor of Alexandria which by purifying itself and
turning again to God is transformed into νοῦς? And the *spiritus*
which, in the spiritual man, unites itself to the Spirit of God, is
actually the πνεῦμα of Origen.

If now, leaving the vocabulary aside, we go to pore over the
texts wherein William describes prayer and those who pray in
each of the "states" mentioned above, we shall still find, in the
midst of a mass of personal and original ideas, the influence of the
great Origen.

The "animal" man does not know how to pray as he should for
he has not the "spirit of God." From time to time such a man prays
from the heart but not with understanding.[79] His God is the God
of Israel, "carnal," who keeps himself "in darkness" (*in caligine*),
in an obscure cloud.[80] Like the ordinary man, or the beginner of
Origen, he is a captive of the "letter"[81] and barely knows Christ
according to the flesh.[82] His religion, entirely centered on the

78. Cf. the *Golden Letter*, no. 198.

79. *Exposition*, nos. 14 and 17; and for Origen, *De Oratione*, chap. II.

80. *Exposition*, the end of no. 14. See H. de Lubac, *Exégèse Médiévale*, vol.
II, part I, pp. 477–478, for the meaning of this expression and its connections
with Origen.

81. *Exposition*, no. 18. The "letter" here is the "formulary of faith," the
"creed."

82. Numerous are the passages in which Origen says of the "simple" that
"they suppose that the Word Incarnate is all of the Word and they know
Christ only according to the flesh" (*In Joan.*, II, 3, 27–31, PG 14: 113; *In Gen.*,
7, 4, PG 12: 201; *In Ezech.*, VII, PG 13: 726–727). Indeed, William clearly
alludes to this state (see nos. 16 and 17) wherein he stresses its absolute validity
but he immediately goes on to show that this contact by faith "with only one
aspect of the Word" normally leads to "the contemplation in Christ, of the
glory of the divine majesty" (cf. no. 28). Likewise, Origen says: "We have
seen him," say the simple faithful, "he had no form nor beauty"; but the
perfect say: "We have seen his glory as of the only Son, full of grace and
truth" (*In Matth.*, XII, 30, PG 13: 1049).

economy of the mystery of the humanity of the Lord (*ea quae sunt humanae dispensationis Christi*), is "simple," still closed to the things of God.[83] But his very fidelity and the attachment he already has for Truth, known "in his obscure secrets, in images and in parables," prepare him for a clearer notion of the Kingdom of God, for the revelation of the Father, "face to face, eye to eye, kiss to kiss."[84]

This revelation will be accomplished when, having "understanding" at the price of laborious efforts, he shall have received the "pledge and dowry" in view of the future espousals;[85] when, purified by the "comings and goings" of Christ, the divine Spouse, he will hold himself in readiness to receive that which lies beyond the realm of science and the "alien kisses"—wisdom, the supreme kiss, received directly from the Word *in Spiritu*.[86]

He does not go so far as to approximate to the point of mergence the "rational" and "spiritual" states—a fact which indicates the limits of Origen's influence on our author.[87]

83. *Exposition*, no. 16. In regard to the expression *humana dispensatio Christi*, see nos. 18, 20, 80, 152. In other respects this text is thoroughly Origenist: "The two Testaments are for her the two breasts of the Bridegroom. From them is to be sucked the milk of all the mysteries accomplished in time (i.e. the letter of the Scriptures), for our eternal salvation, in order to attain to the food which is the Word of God, God with God. For Christ, in his humility (made flesh) is our milk; God equal with God, he is our food. . . . The Bride sucked at the breasts when she first understood (animal state); she remembers the breasts when she meditates on what she has understood (rational state)"—*Exposition*, no. 46.

84. *Exposition*, no. 35.

85. *Exposition*, no. 20, for the expression: "pledge and dowry" (*arrha, sive dos*).

86. *Exposition*, nos. 21 and 36.

87. *Exposition*, no. 22: "rational or spiritual (he is rational in so far as he is guided to his goal by reason, and spiritual in the measure of his attainment once he has attained it)." And in no. 23: "While this man is working out his purification, he is rational; but when he is purified, he is spiritual." And as for Origen, we know that, in practice, he hardly speaks of any other than of the "simple" and the "perfect" (cf. K. Rahner, "Les Débuts d'une Doctrine des Cinq Sens Spirituels chez Origène" in *Revue d'Ascétique et de Mystique*, 1932, pp. 129–131).

But it is now time to come to the *Exposition* properly so called. By the notes and references to be found with my French translation, it can be seen that William in fact follows Origen's *Commentary on the Song of Songs* step by step. Still, it is not possible to pick out everything. Often, it is only a word, an idea of the Alexandrian, that suggests to William a masterly development. How many stimulating images there are, which it would never occur to us to seek out in the involved pages and even in the grandiose imagery of Origen but which we are able to taste and savor in the text of William! Here are a few: the dowry or the pledge of the Spouse (20 and 35); the kisses by proxy received by the ministry of angels, apostles, prophets and doctors (36); the wine of dogma and the venom of false doctrine (38); the gold of the spiritual meaning (72); the youth of the beginners, the soft wax which easily receives the imprint of the Finger of God that is the Holy Spirit (125);[88] the clefts, the fissures in this rock which is Christ and by means of which we attain to God (164).

William, however, has nothing of the plagiarist about him. This is evident when, in returning to the formula of Pope St Gregory the Great which illustrates the theme of his *Exposition on the Song of Songs:* "love itself is knowledge,"[89] he gives it a decidedly personal twist: "love itself is insight" (*amor ipse intellectus est*). Just one word, but how significant.[90]

88. For Origen, see the beautiful texts of his *Commentary on the Epistle to the Romans,* IV, 5, inserted by William into his own *Exposition* on the same Epistle: "Indeed what is of grace is traced in our souls by the Finger of God, that is, the Holy Spirit. The faithful soul, docile to the faith coming from God, gives himself to the Holy Spirit as a well prepared piece of wax to receive whatever he pleases to inscribe upon him; and what has been written upon a man by the love of the Spirit will remain inviolably in his affections forever" (PL 180: 587d).

89. "When we love the heavenly thing we have heard, we know what is loved, because love itself is knowledge."—*Homil. XXVII in Evang.,* 4; PL 76: 1207a.

90. Referring to this liberty of William's in regard to his sources, Father de Lubac gives a typical example apropos Origen's allegory of "The Beautiful

Two of the most beautiful developments of the *Exposition* undoubtedly take their departure from an idea of Origen which is developed until all its richness has been expressed. On the one hand, it concerns the comment on "If you do not know yourself, go out" (*Si non cognoveris te, egredere*) of chapter one, verse eight, and, on the other hand, the theme of the *ordo caritatis* in chapter two, verse four. Origen justifies the "know yourself" of the inspired text by his teaching that the soul is the image of God, and the image of God constitutes "natural beauty" (*decor naturalis*) in it, therefore there exists an *exaequatio* between the soul and its "beauty." To be cognizant of this beauty is, then, for the soul, to know itself and to know God.[91]

William adopts this point of view entirely,[92] but he places it in a setting peculiarly his own. For this he borrows elements from his own mystical psychology and from that of other authors.[93] In it he emphasizes certain traits; he heightens the colors and, in the end, we have a complete picture that is quite William's, a sort of synthesis which leaves the analysis of the Alexandrian far behind.[94] There is, however, not only here and there, but from one end to the other, the same basic idea, even, sometimes, the same words.[95]

Captive," cf. *Exégèse Médiévale*, vol. I, part I, pp. 290–302. In another connection, see the closing lines of no. 3 of William's *Exposition*.

91. *In Cant., l.c.,* 123.

92. See nos. 62, 64 and 66.

93. We will speak of Plotinus in particular a little further on.

94. Origen enlarges, for example, on all the places from which one can go out of oneself (*In Cant., l.c.,* 124a–125a); on the knowledge (above all philosophical knowledge) of God and of the soul (126ab); on the science of the Scriptures which allow the soul to take cognizance of itself and to "get hold" of itself (127). William summarizes all this in a few formulae.

95. In treating of the expression "Go forth and depart" (*jubeo te exire*), Origen sends the soul "to the left with the goats, the lascivious senses" (*sensus lascivos*; 125c), and William does likewise (no. 65), except that he says "lascivious impulses" (*motus lascivos*). "The steps of the flocks" (*vestigia gregum*) is, for the Alexandrian, the sinners or the philosophical sects; for our

The contrast is even more striking where the second tableau is concerned, that of the "ordering of charity" (*ordinatio caritatis*). With Origen it is a course in ethics, containing a wealth of Scripture which is most certainly beautiful but it hardly goes beyond a cold and didactic exposition of the different objects upon which our love can and should be focused.[96] It is simply supported by the numerous texts and examples taken from the Bible.[97] With William, however, it is an ascetical and mystical treatise which could well be entitled: "From the Ill-regulated to the Well-ordered Love of God through Love of Self and Neighbor."[98] "This is the order of charity . . . formed by God in a certain manner in man's natural reason. Hence it is that the judgment of reason discerns this order and the sense of the good will approves it; but without the breath of the grace of the Holy Spirit, the good soul's affection possesses it not" (129).

In itself, love is disordered. It has neither rule nor measure (120). Hence the necessity of "proving" (of "languors" in William's language) by which God cleanses it (121–122). Hence, too, the constraining law that God first imposes upon it: love of neighbor, which serves to tear the soul away from itself (123–128); love of self, rightly ordered, which does not forget the body (128); love of God above all, even to the union of wills and to the "exchange of loves" (130–131)—the summit, here below, of the spiritual life. This is a whole mystical psychology, foreign to Origen, that William introduces. But the influence of the former is manifest in the basic idea, i.e. the putting in order of love by God himself in

---

author it is the "throng who are on their way to perdition," that mass of individuals "who feed themselves and love themselves . . . whose dwelling places (their own) are to all generations" (an allusion to the philosophers).

96. *In Cant., l.c.,* 155ff.

97. *Ibid.,* 158ff.

98. William here makes a résumé of his very first treatise, *On the Nature and Dignity of Love,* and enriches it with new viewpoints.

the heart of man, and even in the harmonics and interwoven themes with which William illustrates his thesis.[99]

Origen's influence is real, profound and beneficial. The Alexandrian has guided our author in his "moral interpretation" of the Song of Songs. From St Bernard, William acquired the art—certainly a great one—of working his own religious and mystical experience into the web of a sacred writing.[100] From Origen, he learned another art, which is no less great, that of uniting—even to the point of identifying—this personal experience, this "adventure" let us call it,[101] with the "adventure" of the Church, Christ's Spouse in exile. He had no other ambition, when setting to work on his Commentary ("restraining ourselves within ourselves and measuring ourselves by ourselves")[102] than to show the onward plodding of his own soul in its movement toward God. And just as he has taken the great Alexandrian Doctor as his guide, as his companion in adventure, so too he has been led to describe for us this "individual soul in the heart of the Church," to show us its "personal union with the Word, as a consequence of the union of Christ with his Church."[103] Universal, because Christian; upheld by theology and founded on dogma, his "experience" seems to us, as it does in Origen, the "moral" that prolongs and supposes the "allegory."[104] And if we see his mystique taking on a "trinitarian" aspect, might it not be yet once more partly indebted to the Christian judgment of Adamantius?

---

99. For example, in this passage: "This is the order of charity ordained by the law of the Spirit of life, proclaimed by the Word of God in the Holy Spirit; written by the finger of God in the heart of him who loves according to right order, and formed by God in a certain manner in man's natural reason."

100. Cf. *supra,* note 14.

101. Cf. *supra,* p. xxv.

102. *Exposition,* no. 5.

103. Cf. H. de Lubac, *Exégèse Médiévale,* vol. 1, part 1, pp. 202–203.

104. *Ibid.*

Saint Augustine

We are far from forgetting, and above all of minimizing, the influence of the Latin doctors, St Gregory and St Augustine, on William's thinking and affective mysticism. It has been said that the latter of the two was "perhaps his favorite author."[105] The "perhaps" is not an exaggeration and it is certain that among the identifiable sources used by our author, the gamut of the writings of the Doctor of Hippo is in the ascendancy. William sees him as the "Doctor of Grace" and several times in his *Exposition on the Epistle to the Romans* it is to him that he has recourse in order to complete or rectify a text or a concept of Origen.[106]

It has recently been demonstrated[107] that the *Enigma of Faith* or treatise *On the Trinity*, which owes so much to Scotus Eriugena for its speculative aspect, follows, in general, the Augustinian point of

105. J. Hourlier, *The Works of William of St Thierry*, vol. 1, Introduction.

106. Here is a typical example. Regarding Jacob and Esau (Rom 9:10–11) William writes, citing Origen (*In Rom.*, VII, 15; PG 14: 1143a): "We teach that it is not the sons of the flesh but the sons (of God) who are the seed; as Isaac was chosen, the younger of the two, that he should be the adopted son of God, so it is true that the promises of God are not with the sons according to flesh but with the sons of God, and not due to works (here it is St Augustine who is speaking!—*Ep. ad Sixt.*, 195, 34) but to the call of grace, according to God's choice which remains not with the sons of the flesh but the sons of God" (PL 180: 646bc). The last words refer to the text of Origen, but it is certain that William, in allowing St Augustine to have a word, wanted to insist on the intervention of a purely gratuitous grace in the choice of God, an intervention that Origen himself had pointed out in the foregoing. He takes his inspiration from treatise twenty-seven of St Augustine on St John, no. 2 ff., which, moreover, he quotes explicitly a few lines further on: "Why is this one drawn and that one not drawn, these are the hidden things of the Son; do not wish to inquire if you do not wish to err. If you are not drawn, pray that you might be drawn" (*ibid.*, 562d).

107. See Dom Odo Brooke OSB, *The Trinity in Guillaume de Saint Thierry Against the Anthropological Background of his Doctrine of the Ascent of the Soul to God* (typewritten thesis), Rome, 1957. Some important extracts have appeared in *Recherches de Théologie Ancienne et Médiévale*, 26 (1959), pp. 85–127; 27 (1960), pp. 193–211; 28 (1961), pp. 26–58.

view;[108] though it does not entirely neglect the theory of the psychological analysis of the Trinity in man, especially in the place it gives to the Holy Spirit in trinitarian economy and in man's return to the triune God in whose image he is made. From the very first pages of this important work the thesis is posited:

> In the divine Trinity the Father and the Son see each other mutually and for them to see each other mutually is to be "one." But man finds himself called to see God some day as he is and, seeing him, to become like him. And just as between the Father and the Son there is unity where there is vision, so too between man and God there will be likeness where there is vision. Now the unity of the Father and the Son is the Holy Spirit. It is, therefore, he who is the love and who will be man's likeness to God.[109]

From this text[110] we have extracted a fundamental proposition which is clearly Augustinian, namely, that the Holy Spirit is the

108. This is contrary to what I have written in *Guillaume de Saint-Thierry, L'homme et son Oeuvre,* p. 109. I must reverse my conclusion: Augustinian climate in general with Oriental influences which are quite numerous.

109. "There (where God is seen as he is, face to face; where there is such great excellence that much more is attained by charity than either faith believed or hope desired) just as in the Trinity which is God, the Father and Son mutually see each other, and mutually see that they are one and that the one is what the other is, so the predestined who are taken to God will see God as he is and by seeing they will become as he is, be like him. There just as the vision shared by the Father and the Son is unity itself, so the vision shared by God and man will be the likeness itself. The Holy Spirit, the unity of the Father and the Son, is charity and the likeness of God in man"—*Aenigma Fidei,* PL 180: 399cd. It is, then, a matter of the "face-to-face vision," comparable to the "vision" of the Father and the Son. But we know that something of this "vision" is accorded to man by way of anticipation, "to those to whom the Father and the Son communicate the Holy Spirit more abundantly (*largiuntur*) along with their mutual knowledge and their mutual will"— *Mirror of Faith,* PL 180: 393a. We shall not dwell upon the problem posed by the connection of "vision" to "likeness"; it has already been done elsewhere: cf. J. M. Déchanet, "Amor intellectus est" in *Revue du Moyen Age Latin,* I (1955), pp. 352–354 and note 9.

110. Even more with respect to the other texts of the *Mirror of Faith* and of the *Exposition* to which we shall return further on.

unity of the Father and the Son,[111] or, what amounts to the same thing, he is the Spirit of the One and the Other,[112] the Love that joins them together,[113] their ineffable Communion,[114] their Holiness, their Charity.[115] Breaking with the traditional doctrine[116] which had found its expression in the consecrated formula *ex Patre, per Filium, in Spiritu Sancto,* and which shows us the Spirit proceeding *from* the Father, *through* the Son—the divinity flowing from the Father, through the Son to the Holy Spirit—the theology of St Augustine displaces, if we may so express it, the principle of unity in the divine Trinity, moving it from the Father to the Holy Spirit

111. *Unitas amborum—De Trinitate,* VI, 5, 7.

112. "The Holy Spirit is the Spirit of the Father and the Son" (*Spiritus sanctus et Patris et Filii spiritus est—De Trin.,* V, 11, 12); "the Spirit common to both" (*qui spiritus est communis ambobus—De Trin.,* XV, 19, 37).

113. "That perfect charity which joins them together" (*summa caritas utrumque conjungens—De Trin,* VII, 3, 6); "the substantial and consubstantial love of both" (*caritas substantialis et consubstantialis ambobus—In Joan.,* CV, 3).

114. "The ineffable communion of the Father and the Son" (*ineffabilis est quaedam Patris Filioque communio—De Trin.,* V, 11, 12).

115. "For whether the Holy Spirit is the unity between both of them, or their holiness, or their love . . ." (*sive enim Spiritus sanctus sit unitas amborum, sive sanctitas, sive caritas . . .—De Trin.,* VI, 5, 7). "And if the love by which the Father loves the Son and the Son loves the Father is an ineffable revelation of the love between the two, what is more fitting than that he who is the Spirit and common to both should rightly be called love?" (*Si caritas qua Pater diligit Filium et Patrem diligit Filius ineffabiliter communionem demonstrat amborum, quid convenientius quam ut ille dicatur caritas proprie, qui Spiritus est communis ambobus?—De Trin.,* XV, 19, 37).

116. The *Theological Sermons* of St Gregory Nazianzus, quoted by V. Lossky, *Essai sur la Théologie Mystique de l'Eglise d'Orient* (Paris, 1944), pp. 44–61, can give some idea of this doctrine. There are also certain similar passages in the *Treatise on the Holy Spirit* of Basil of Caesarea: "The Holy Spirit, like the Father is *one;* he binds himself through the *one* Son to the *one* Father; and through himself he brings to completion the Blessed Trinity" (c. XVIII; PG 32: 152a). "In the divine nature which is simple, it is in the communication of the Deity, from the Father to the Spirit through the Son, that unity resides" (*ibid.,* 149c). "The essential goodness, the natural holiness, the royal dignity flow from the Father, through the Only-Begotten, to the Spirit" (*ibid.,* 153bc).

by making him the "substantial bond" between the two other persons, the interior bond of the whole Trinity.

It is interesting to see how our author adopts St Augustine's point of view integrally, while still respecting the traditional schema and presenting to us the Father as the "Source and Origin of the divinity, the Principle of the Son and the Spirit who come from him and receive from him that which they are."[117] Our prayers are addressed to the Father, through the Son, in the Holy Spirit,[118] but the Holy Spirit is none the less the Spirit of the Father and the Son. He proceeds from the One and the Other for he is the charity and the unity of the One and the Other.[119] This is why, moreover, in so far as he is the love of the Father and the Son, the reciprocal gift of the One to the Other, he is called the "Gift of God." As Charity in relation to the Father and the Son, he becomes, in his temporal mission, the one who extends toward the creature this eternal relation, both as the love of God for man and the love of man for God[120].

This is a second Augustinian proposition, a corollary of the first,

117. *Est enim Deus Pater quasi fons quidam et origo Divinitatis, principium Filii et Spiritus Sancti, qui ab ipso sunt, ab ipso habentes esse quod sunt—Aenigma Fidei*, PL 180: 435d.

118. "For we pray and adore, and give thanks to the Father, always with the Son and the Holy Spirit; and nevertheless through the Son as through the mediator between God and man, our Lord, Jesus Christ, in the Holy Spirit, our Paraclete and the Advocate of our prayers before God."—*Aenigma Fidei*, PL 180: 436a.

119. "Since he is the Holy Spirit, the Spirit of the Father and the Son, and proceeding from them, and their charity, it is clear that he is not one of these two"—*ibid.*, 439c. William takes his inspiration from St Augustine, *De Trin.*, VI, 5, 7.

120. "The Holy Spirit is properly called Gift because of charity"—*Aenigma Fidei*, PL 180, 440a, and St Augustine, *De Trin.*, XV, 18, 32. This is true *ad extra* (the gift of the Spirit to men by diffusion of charity in their hearts) but equally so *ad intra*: "In their own proper gift, they [the Father and the Son] preserve their unity in spirit in a bond of peace" (*Suo proprio dono [Pater et Filius] servant unitatem spiritu in vinculo pacis*), wrote St Augustine (*De Trin.*, VI, 5, 7) in a passage reproduced by William (*Aenigma*, 439c).

which in the *Enigma* forms the basis for the theology of the Spirit but which in the treatise *On Contemplating God*[121] appears as the key doctrine of William's already clearly trinitarian spirituality and which, in his last works, supports and justifies his theory of "love-knowledge."

It is because he is, consubstantially and naturally, the mutual charity, unity, resemblance and knowledge of the Father and the Son, that once given to man, the Holy Spirit produces by his presence this charity, this unity, this resemblance, this knowledge in the faithful soul which he fashions into his temple.[122] And the latter, in some way held in the embrace and kiss of the Father and the Son, with blissful awareness,[123] finds itself a participant of the knowledge that they have of each other.

The road to the knowledge of God, say the Greek Fathers,[124] leads from the Spirit, through the Son, to the Father—once the Charity of God has been diffused in our hearts by the gift of the Holy Spirit. "In the Spirit" (*in Spiritu*), according to the traditional economy, is the preparatory stage for contact with Christ who reveals the Father. William reverses this order: *in Spiritu*—"in the Spirit"—is, for him, sort of a goal.[125] The soul is first of all the bride

121. See the Introduction of J. Hourlier, *l.c.*

122. "There (in the divine substance) the Holy Spirit is naturally and consubstantially unity, likeness and knowledge; here (in man) be brings it about that they exist. . . . There unity is the mutual knowledge of the Father and the Son; here it is the likeness of man to God."—*Mirror of Faith*, PL 180: 393b.

123. "Man in some way finds himself in the midst of that embrace and kiss of the Father and Son, who is the Holy Spirit"—*ibid.*, 394b. "The blessed conscience in some way finds itself in the embrace and kiss of the Father and Son"—*Golden Letter*, no. 263.

124. Cf. Basil of Caesarea, "*Traité du Saint-Esprit*," XVIII, *Sources Chrétiennes*, 17, p. 197.

125. "In the traditional economy, *in Spiritu* is preparation for receiving Christ (*per Filium*), the Holy Spirit being the initial point of contact which leads us to Christ. Guillaume reverses this order, while at the same time preserving the formula of the traditional economy. The initial stage is not *in Spiritu* but *per Filium*; with special reference to the Incarnation. The final

of the Word. After having come into contact "with something of Christ" (the animal state), she is "introduced first into the cellars of the divine King."[126] Then, after many purifications and inducements to love (the rational state), she is led into the "cellar of wine." There the mystical union is consummated; the soul is plunged into the Holy Spirit (the spiritual state):

> Upon this bed takes place that wonderful union and mutual fruition—of sweetness, and of joy incomprehensible and inconceivable even to those in whom it takes place—between man and God, the created spirit and the Uncreated. They are named Bride and Bridegroom, while words are sought that may some-

---

stage is *in Spiritu*. *In Spiritu* implies the whole doctrine of the Holy Ghost as the mutual union of the Father and the Son, and the source of our participated union" (O. Brooke, *The Trinity in Guillaume de Saint-Thierry*, p. 210). It can be noted that William is well in accord with traditional theology, and with that of the Greek Fathers in particular, when he makes the Holy Spirit the "bond of union" between God and man. Commenting, for example, in the *Golden Letter*, on the *in Spiritu* of St Paul (2 Cor 6:6) he writes: "See how he places, in the midst of the virtues, like the heart in the body, that Holy Spirit, the author, the arranger, the vivifier of all things. He is the all-powerful Artisan who produces man's good will towards God, and God's reconciliation with man. . . . May men teach the search for God, and the angels the adoration of him! Only from the Holy Spirit can we learn to find him, to possess him, to enjoy him."—*Golden Letter*, nos. 264-266. The Holy Spirit is indeed, then, the "instrument" of the knowledge of God, with William as with the Greek Fathers. The sole difference, notes Dom Brooke, lies in the *how* and especially the *why* of his intervention: "The only difference lies in the reason *why* the Holy Ghost is the *bond of union*" (*l.c.*, p. 193). With the Greeks, it is the Spirit who "completes the Holy Trinity" (the Divinity coming down from the Father to him through the Son), communicates himself to men and leads them (in a re-ascending movement) "through the Son" to the Father. With William, it is because, being the bond of union between the Father and the Son, once given to men "by the Son," he "becomes, in his way, for man in regard to God, what in virtue of the consubstantial union, he is for the Son with regard to the Father and for the Father with regard to the Son" (*Golden Letter*, no. 263). One can only admire the logic and the continuity of William's doctrine, based on the Augustine point of view, which he has made his own and re-thought completely.

126. *Exposition on the Song of Songs*, no. 95.

how express in human language the charm and sweetness of this union, which is nothing else than the unity of the Father and the Son of God, their Kiss, their Embrace, their Love, their Goodness and whatever in that supremely simple Unity is common to both. All this is the Holy Spirit—God, Charity, at once Giver and Gift. Upon this bed are exchanged that kiss and that embrace by which the Bride begins to know as she herself is known. And as happens in the kisses of lovers, who by a certain sweet, mutual exchange, impart their spirit each to the other, so the created spirit pours itself out wholly into the Spirit who creates it for this very effusion; and the Creator Spirit infuses himself into it as he wills, and man becomes one spirit with God. . . .

But the welcoming breast of love, opening yet wider to meet your magnitude, while it loves you or aspires to love you in all your greatness, grasps the ungraspable and comprehends the incomprehensible. But what am I saying: "It grasps"? Nay rather, it is very Love (and you are Love) that grasps—it is you Holy Spirit, O Father, who proceeds from you and from the Son, with whom you and the Son are one.[127]

Plenitude of the Word; plenitude of the Spirit; *in him* the clear revelation of the Father; *per Filium, in Spiritu, ad Patrem*—this is the theme of the entire *Exposition*. After having shown what the theory of the three states and his interpretation of the *Song of Songs* owe to the genius of Origen, it is only right to emphasize what the mystical psychology of William with regard to his trinitarian theology owes to this other Western genius, St Augustine.

The Doctor of Hippo is also represented in the *Exposition* by several secondary themes: the theory of the virtues of pagans, for example, or, again, the memory-understanding-love concept of the divine image.[128] We must not stop here. St Gregory of Nyssa suggests to William a double etymology of the word *Deus*[129] as it comes down to us through Scotus Eriugena whose terminology is recognizable a little further on in connection with "theophanies" or divine manifestations.[130]

---

127. *Exposition*, no. 100.
129. *Exposition*, no. 152.

128. *Exposition*, no. 105, see also no. 76.
130. *Exposition*, no. 153.

Plotinus

No less certain and even more important is the influence of Plotinus on the thought and vocabulary of our author. A happy theme, that of the "land of unlikeness" (*regio dissimilitudinis*),[131] occurs twice in the *Exposition* and each time under a form indicating two different sources. The first time William writes: "Go . . . to the place of unlikeness" (*Abi . . . in locum dissimilitudinis*),[132] which is a literal translation of Plotinus. We must not be surprised at this as the context is quite reminiscent of that of many of the *Enneads*. The second time, he shows us the soul as having fallen "into such an abyss of unlikeness that no hope was left" (*in tantum profundum dissimilitudinis, ut nulla spes esset*).[133] This passage calls to mind at once Plato (in a translation of Proclus) and Plotinus.[134] Again, Plotinus is used to press his point in a curious application of a Pauline verse to the theme of the soul drawn into itself, purified, cleaving to the One.[135]

Finally, let us not forget that this same Plotinus is one of the obvious sources of the love-knowledge theory of our author. If St Gregory provided the idea for the nice turn of phrase: "love itself is insight" (*amor ipse intellectus est*), and St Augustine suggested the theology that supports and, in a sense, forms the basis of William's mystical psychology, the point of departure for this psychology is none the less undoubtedly "Plotinian." It is found in the very clear affirmation of the *Enneads* that there are in man something like two principles of knowledge: the νοῦς which

131. See F. Chatillon, "Regio Dissimilitudinis" in *Mélanges Podechard* (Lyons, 1945), pp. 85–102, and G. Dumeige's article "Dissemblence" in *Dict. de Spiritualité*, vol. III, col. 1336–1338.

132. *Exposition*, no. 65.

133. *Exposition*, no. 83.

134. See J. M. Déchanet, "Guillaume et Plotin" in *Revue du Moyen Age Latin*, 2 (1946), pp. 246–247 and note 10.

135. *Exposition*, no. 147; cf. "Guillaume et Plotin," *l.c.*, p. 256.

reasons (the *intellectus* or *animus* of William) and the νοῦς transported by love.[136] This is not quite the Plotinian ecstasy which may have provided William with some elements from which to choose; for example, the image of the lover who desires to melt into the beloved[137] or, still better, the fusion of the soul and of the good to the point of being completely indistinguishable.[138] From this William will form his *unitas spiritus* by bringing to this concept certain necessary precisions.

By way of conclusion to this study it can be said that we do not know what to admire more: William's eclecticism or his theological insight that permits him to make a synthesis of elements and thoughts so assuredly diverse. We have in the *Exposition* a work of quality, traditional yet original, wherein the experience of a saint joins the working theories of the great doctors of the Church—Gregory, Origen, Augustine—and which does not fear to clothe itself with the spoils of Egypt!

J. M. Déchanet OSB

---

136. See the collected texts in "Guillaume et Plotin," *l.c.*, pp. 250–252.

137. *Enneads*, VI, 7, 34. Cf. "Guillaume et Plotin," *l.c.*, p. 253.

138. *Enneads, ibid.*, and again, VI, 7, 31. For William, cf. the *Mirror of Faith*, PL 180: 390cd and 394a. See especially the *Golden Letter*, no. 263. In regard to ecstasy (in the Plotinian sense) this passage (no. 268) is significant: "To the elect of God there is shown, from time to time, some reflection of the face of God, after the manner of a light which appears and disappears by turns." Plotinus wrote in the *Enneads*, V, 5, 8: "a light would suddenly appear ... which at one time would show itself and at another time would not show itself"; "a faint glimmer which arouses the desire for the fullness of light" (*Enneads*, VI, 7, 33); "this fleeting glimpse inflames the soul with the desire to possess the full vision of eternal light" (*Golden Letter, ibid.*).

EXPOSITION ON
THE SONG OF SONGS

PREFACE

O LORD our God, you did create us to your image and likeness,[1] it is plain, that we might contemplate you and have
fruition of you. No one who contemplates you reaches
fruition of you save insofar as he becomes like to you.[2] O splendor of
the highest Good, you ravish with desire of you every rational soul;
the more a soul burns for you, the purer it is in itself; the purer it is,
the freer it is from bodily things to turn rather to spiritual things.
Free then from the servitude of corruption that inner force of ours
which ought to serve you alone: I mean by this our love. For it is

1. Cf. Gen. 1:26: "We have made man to our image and likeness." This
is a fundamental text in regard to the whole of Cistercian mysticism; it is
not by chance that it stands at the beginning of this exposition. For an excellent study of this, see A. Hallier, *The Monastic Theology of Aelred of
Rievaulx* (Cistercian Studies Series, 2), ch. 1. In these notes we will seek to
bring out some of the more common themes to be found in the writings of the
Cistercian Fathers by indicating parallels in William himself and in other
Cistercians, especially Bernard of Clairvaux. In the very useful notes appended
to the French translation, published in the *Sources Chrétiennes* series, Dom
Déchanet has indicated the considerable influence which the tradition started
by Origen has had upon the Cistercians in their commentaries on the *Song
of Songs*. Cf. Guillaume de Saint-Thierry, *Exposé sur le Cantique des Cantiques*
(Paris: Les Editions du Cerf, 1962).—William uses the words of the Sacred
Text quite extensively in his writings, although perhaps not so abundantly
and obviously as Bernard and Aelred and some of the other writers of the
Cistercian school. We will, therefore, not attempt to cite all the scriptural
phrases or allusions to be found in this *Exposition*, but only the more significant
ones.

2. Cf. 1 Jn 3:2: "We will be like him, when we see him as he is." Another
fundamental text which is interpreted by underlining the reciprocity of the
influence of the vision on the resemblance and of the resemblance on the
vision.

love that, when it is free, makes us like to you, to the degree in
which we are drawn to you by the sense of life. And through this
whoever lives by the Spirit of life[3] experiences you. Such a one, as
the Apostle says, beholding the glory of the Lord with open face,
is transformed into the same image from glory to glory as by the
Spirit of the Lord.[4]

2. For when we love any creature, not to use it for you but to
enjoy it in itself, love becomes not love but greed or lust or something of the kind, losing with the loss of freedom even the grace
of the name of love. And man, in his misery, is compared to sense-
less beasts and is become like to them.[5] And his whole sin consists
in enjoying amiss and using amiss, for that is what he does when
he loves some object, or his neighbor or himself not, as we said,
to use it for you but to enjoy it in itself. Although it is permitted
him to enjoy both his neighbor and himself, he must not do so save
in you—in you who are the life of all lives and the good of all
goods, both in yourself and in him. And this is living and luminous
love, which is free, and which frees from corruption. The purer it
is, the sweeter; the stronger it is in its affection, the more constant

3. "Sense of life—Spirit of life" (*sensus vitae—Spiritus vitae*). *Infra,* no. 67,
we find these two expressions brought into relation with one another: "The
sense of life from the Spirit of life discloses it" (*Sensus vitae de Spiritu vitae
indicat hoc*). William presents love to us as an experience by which the soul
experiences whatever it experiences of God by the Spirit of life—*sentit quidquid
de Deo secundum Spiritum vitae sentit*—the Spirit of life being the Holy Spirit
himself. See also William's *Mirror of Faith,* where he speaks of the wisdom of
God by which God is savored by the wise man, who lives by the Spirit of
life even to the experience of his love: *qua sapit Deus sapienti; viventi de Spiritu
vitae eius usque ad sensum amoris eius* (PL 180: 385; trans. G. Webb and A.
Walker [London: Mowbray, 1959], p. 50).

4. Cf. 2 Cor 3:18 and the passage in the *Mirror of Faith* where this same text
is used to illustrate the role of transforming love in the vision and knowledge
of God, trans. Webb and Walker, p. 60; cf. also *Meditations,* 3, trans. Sr
Penelope, in *The Works of William of St Thierry,* vol. 1 (Cistercian Fathers
Series 3).

5. Cf. Ps 48:13. (The *Vulgate* enumeration of the psalms is used throughout
s being that with which William was familiar.)

in its effect. Through godliness it grows sweet in the conscience, but through justice it waxes strong in the work it undertakes.

3. Set love free in us, O Lord, that your Bride, the Christian soul, dowered with your blood and possessed of the pledge of your Spirit, may love you chastely and sing you her love songs amid the grievous sufferings of this life,[6] in the weariness of her pilgrimage far from you and her prolonged sojourn[7] in a strange land. Then may she be refreshed and find her pain lighter. May she be drawn to cleave to you and in the meantime forget where she is. May she hear something whereby she may understand what is wanting to her.[8] It is time now to have mercy on her, the time now is come,[9] when you have allured her and led her into the wilderness that there you might speak to her heart.[10]

Speak therefore and say to her and to her heart, "I am your salvation."[11] Speak that she may hear. Inspire her that she may feel. Give that she may possess, that all that is within her may bless you[12] and all her bones may say to you, "Lord, who is like to you?"[13] You, O Lord, are her helper and protector.[14] By this conversation which she holds alone with you, may the multitude who say to her, "There is no salvation for her in her God,"[15] be greatly confounded. By conversation with you, let love come into being if it exists not already. If it does exist, may it increase and gain in strength until your handmaid, taken prisoner by right of war and chosen by the lot of victory, finds grace in your eyes through bringing forth fruit worthy of penance.[16] When everything her being can spare has been cut away by you according to the law, let her pass over into the embrace of the Victor in everlasting charity and indissoluble union.

6. Cf. Ps 136:4.
8. Cf. Ps 38:5.
10. Cf. Hos 2:14.
12. Cf. Ps 102:1.
14. Cf. Ps 118:114.
16. Cf. Mt 3:8.

7. Cf. Ps 119:5.
9. Cf. Ps 101:14.
11. Ps 34:3.
13. Cf. Ps 34:10.
15. Ps 3:3.

4. This is why, as we set about the task of pondering the epithalamium—the nuptial canticle, the song of bridegroom and bride—and examining your work, we beseech you, O Holy Spirit, that we may be filled, O Love, with your love, in order to understand the canticle of love. Thus may we also become in some measure participants in the holy conversation of Bridegroom and Bride, that what we read may take effect within us. For where affections are concerned, only persons possessing like affections can readily understand what is said.[17]

Draw us therefore unto yourself, O Holy Spirit; O Holy Paraclete, O Holy Comforter,[18] comfort the poverty of our solitude which seeks no solace apart from you.[19] Enlighten and quicken the

17. As one reads the opening paragraph of St Bernard's Seventy-ninth Sermon on the Song of Songs one cannot help but wonder if he perhaps had these opening paragraphs of William's *Exposition* in mind, for the thought is very similar. To quote but a sentence or two: "It is love that is speaking everywhere. And should any one of you desire to attain to an understanding of things which he reads, let him love. For it is useless for him who loves not, to attempt to read or listen to this Canticle of love. . . ."

18. William's devotion to the Holy Spirit is manifest throughout his writings; see e.g. the peroration of his *Enigma of Faith*, the *Letter to the Carthusians of Mont Dieu*, no. 63 (trans. W. Shewring, *The Golden Epistle of Abbot William of St Thierry to the Carthusians of Mont Dieu* [London: Sheed & Ward, 1930], pp. 108f. In these notes we will cite the *Letter* according to the paragraph numbers used in this translation; however it should be noted that they are somewhat different in the last part from those in Mabillon's text and also from those used in the new critical Latin edition prepared by Dom Déchanet which will serve as the basis for the English translation to appear in the present Cistercian Fathers Series), and Meditation 6, as well as the analytic index *infra*.

19. Solitude was something which was very precious to William of St Thierry. He will return to it frequently in the *Exposition* (see *infra*, nos. 147, 166, 182, 187). He was convinced that it was a necessary means to attain to the perfection of wisdom and the fullness of contemplation (see *infra*, nos. 28, 61). It was a question of external solitude being essential to arrive at the more important and true solitude of heart (see *infra*, nos. 28, 106, 160; also *On Contemplating God*, no. 12, trans. Sr Penelope, in *The Works of William of St Thierry*, vol. 1 (Cistercian Fathers Series 3). But William readily acknowledged that not all solitude was good; indeed, solitude without God

desire of him who tends toward you, that it may become the love of one having fruition of you. Come to us that we may truly love you, that whatever we think and say may flow from the fountainhead of your love. May the canticle of your love be read by us in such wise as to kindle in us love itself. Yes, may love itself show us the meaning of its own canticle.

5. We do not presume to treat of those deeper mysteries the Song of Songs contains with regard to Christ and the Church; but restraining ourselves within ourselves and measuring ourselves by ourselves, in the poverty of our understanding we shall (as anyone may venture to do) touch lightly on a certain moral sense apropos of Bridegroom and Bride, Christ and the Christian soul.[20] And we ask for our labor no other reward than one like to our subject, namely, love itself.

6. This book of King Solomon's, then, is entitled the *Song of Songs,* perhaps because, by the grandeur of its thoughts and the pre-eminence of its subject, it seems to surpass all the ancient

---

was fearful and miserable (see *infra,* nos. 105, 188; also *Letter to the Carthusians of Mont Dieu,* no. 9, trans. Shewring, pp. 20f.). He longed for solitude (cf. Meditation 4) and it was for this that he laid down his abbatial burden and went to the Cistercians, for solitude was an essential element of their renewal (cf. *Little Exordium,* ch. 15, trans. R. Larkin, in L. Lekai, *The White Monks* [Okauchee, Wisconsin: Cistercian Fathers, 1953], pp. 262ff.).—St Bernard has an especially beautiful passage on solitude in his Fortieth Sermon on the Song of Songs, no. 4 (trans. K. Walsh, in *The Works of Bernard of Clairvaux,* vol. 3 (Cistercian Fathers Series 7). Cf. also the interesting passage in Helinand of Froidmont, First Sermon for Christmas (PL 212: 489).

20. St Bernard in his *Sermons on the Song of Songs* did not hesitate to touch upon the "deeper mysteries" (see e.g. Sermons 21, 26, 27, 62, 68, etc.) but his predilection was for the moral sense (see especially Sermon 80, no. 1), for as he said: "My purpose is not so much to comment on words as to move and kindle hearts"—Sermon 16, no. 1. Although often enjoying very high forms of contemplation based on solid dogma, the Cistercian Fathers generally were very practical men concerned with the basic moral instruction that one needed to prepare for this gift of contemplation. Cf. also, Guerric of Igny, Sermon for Rogation Days, nos. 4ff., in *The Liturgical Sermons of Guerric of Igny* (Cistercian Fathers Series 32).

canticles of the patriarchs and prophets, for it deals with Bridegroom and Bride, Christ and the rational soul.

Or again, it may be so entitled because it is sung with the accord of holy affections by the blessed people that knows jubilation and walks in the light of God's countenance,[21] rather than chanted with the harmony of voices singing different notes. For this canticle deals with the love of God—the love whereby God is loved, or the love whereby God himself is called Love. Whether we call it love or charity or dilection matters not, except that the word "love" seems to indicate a certain tender affection on the part of the lover with the implication of striving or soliciting; "charity," a certain spiritual affection or the joy of one who has fruition; and "dilection," a natural desire for an object which gives delight. But all these things one and the same Spirit works in the love of Bridegroom and Bride. To sing the new canticle,[22] the movements of all the holy virtues are indeed so useful to the love of Bridegroom and Bride that (granted due and orderly progress of the said virtues) they are all transformed finally into acts of love. Other things shall certainly be made void, but "charity never fails."[23]

7. Or, to give a third reason, the book is entitled the *Song of Songs* because it seems to comprise in itself four songs. It is in fact divided into four parts,[24] each of which ends with the repose, that is, the union of Bridegroom and Bride. This union, out of reverence for the great sacrament in Christ and the Church, the Holy Spirit was pleased to honor with the aforesaid nobler name, calling it repose rather than anything suggestive of carnal relationship. For the Bride says, "While the king was at his repose, my spikenard sent forth its fragrance."[25] At the end of each part of the book, this repose is preceded by its epithalamium (the nuptial canticle with which Bridegroom and Bride are led, as it were, to the bride chamber); and it concludes with peace and assured tranquillity being

21. Cf. Ps 88:16.
22. Cf. Ps 39:4; 143:9; 149:1; Is 42:10; Rev 5:9; 14:3.
23. 1 Cor 13:8.   24. Cf. Introd., pp. xiv f.   25. Song 1:11.

given the Bride by the Bridegroom's power, as she rests in his embrace. At this moment he calls for an oath and says, "I have entreated you, ye daughters of Jerusalem, that you stir not up nor make the beloved to awake till she please."[26] The fourth and last repose, however, would seem to be concluded differently by a loftier mystery. For although the earlier passages appear to hymn the joy of the union of Bridegroom and Bride as a festival, this final one ends when the Bridegroom is strongly urged by the Bride to take flight. She cries aloud and says, "Flee away, O my Beloved, and be like to the roe and to the young hart!"[27] The meaning of this will be set forth in its place if the Bridegroom himself deigns to reveal it.

8. Now this song is written in the manner of a drama and in dialogue style, as if to be recited by characters and with action. Just as various characters and various actions appear in the recitation of dramas, so in this song characters and affections seem to combine to carry through this trafficking of love and the mystical contract of the union of God and man. The characters or groups of characters here are four: the Bridegroom and his companions, and the Bride and the chorus of young maidens. The Bridegroom's companions are the angels, who rejoice with us in our good deeds and love to serve us therein with due ministrations. The maidens, in turn, are tender young souls, who have given their names to the tutelage and profession of spiritual love. By obedient humility and attentive imitation they gladly join themselves to the Bride, in other words, to the company of more perfect souls. The whole action of love, however, is left to the lovers. Thus while their fellow lovers keep silence, stand still, listen and rejoice with joy at the voice of Bridegroom[28] and Bride, scarcely any voice is heard or any utterance repeated in the course of this whole canticle save those of Bridegroom and Bride.

26. Song 2:7; 3:5; 8:4.   27. Song 8:14.   28. Cf. Jn 3:29.

9. Now the argument of the historical drama, tale or parable proposed, may be stated as follows. King Solomon took to wife the daughter of the Pharaoh of Egypt.[29] At first he granted her certain favors of the bridal bed and of love and of the kiss. Then, after having shown her part of his riches and part of his glory, he cast her forth from their mutual union and the favor of the kiss until, by riddance of her Egyptian blackness and rejection of the customs of a barbarous nation, she might become worthy of access to the royal bridechamber.[30]

10. But the spiritual sense is this.[31] When the soul has been converted to God and is to be espoused to the Word of God, at first she is taught to understand the riches of prevenient grace and allowed to "taste and see how sweet the Lord is;"[32] but afterwards she is sent back into the house of her conscience to be instructed, purified in the obedience of charity, perfectly cleansed of vices and richly adorned with virtues, that she may be found worthy of access to the spiritual grace of godliness and affection for virtues which is the bridechamber of the Bridegroom.

11. It was needful to begin with this preamble that thereafter we might hasten by the quickest way after the Bridegroom, allured by the fragrance of his perfumes.[33] First, however, we lay it down as a condition that, should something lovely along the roadside now and then draw us to gaze upon it a little too curiously, this may not offend him who journeys at our side.

12. One last word before we undertake the journey we have proposed. All the parts of this canticle correspond to the different

29. 1 Kings 3:1.

30. *Infra,* no. 146, William explains this more fully and indicates that he bases his historical interpretation on the Books of Paralipomenon. Cf. 2 Chron 8:11.

31. This practice of tracing out first the historical sense and then going on to the spiritual sense, which William will repeat at the beginning of the Second Song (cf. *infra,* no. 146), is prevalent in St Bernard's *Sermons on the Song of Songs* (e.g., Sermons 30, 42, 46, 51, 58, 59, 60, etc.).

32. Ps 33:9.   33. Cf. Song 1:3.

states of men of prayer, or to the forms, causes or subjects of prayer. Hence it seems necessary to give some explanations about the various manners of prayer, so that when the studious and devout reader comes across them as he peruses the holy canticle, he may always revert to himself and recognize them in his own heart.

13. It is evident that there are three states of men of prayer or three states of prayer: animal, rational and spiritual.[34] Every man forms the Lord his God for himself, or sets him before himself, after his own manner. For as the man of prayer himself is, so the God to whom he prays appears to him. And, when a man prays faithfully, on the one hand he always endeavors in the prayer he offers

34. The threefold division of the stages of the spiritual life has been common among Christian authors since the time of Origen who considered three distinct catagories: beginners or "psychics," those making progress or "gnostics," and the perfect or "pneumatics." This threefold division is common among the Cistercian Fathers. Bernard has a very close parallel to William in his Twentieth Sermon on the Song of Songs where he speaks of carnal, rational and spiritual love (cf. trans. K. Walsh, in *The Works of Bernard of Clairvaux*, vol. 2 [Cistercian Fathers Series, 4]). At other times he uses other analogies such as the three cellars in Sermon Twenty-three, or the threefold growth in charity (giving all for love, spontaneous love to all our neighbors, doing good to those who hate us) in Sermon Twenty-seven, or the three degrees of truth (the labor of humility, the affection of compassion, and the ecstasy of contemplation) in *The Steps of Humility*, chs. 4ff. (trans. G. Webb and A. Walker London: [Mowbray, 1957], pp. 33ff.). Aelred of Rievaulx speaks of three sabbaths; cf. *Mirror of Charity*, III, chs. 1f. (trans. G. Webb and A. Walker [London: Mowbray, 1962], pp. 80ff.). Isaac of Stella speaks of three sacrifices: of penance marked by compunction, of justice marked by devotion, of understanding marked by contemplation; see *Letter on the Mass* (PL 194: 1892). Sometimes, however, they used other divisions, e.g. St Bernard's sevenfold infusion of the Holy Spirit in Sermon Eighteen on the Song of Songs, or the twelve steps of humility following St Benedict in *The Steps of Humility*, or the four stages of organic growth: the vine of faith, the branches of virtue, the grapes of good works, the wine of devotion, in Sermon Thirty on the Song of Songs.—William develops his three states, the state of beginners, those advancing and those who are perfect, in his *Letter to the Carthusians of Mont Dieu* (nos. 12ff. and *passim*), using the same terminology as here: animal, rational, spiritual. In his first book, *On the Nature and Dignity of Love,* he developed them under the concept of adolescent love, adult love and full maturity.

to bring God something that is genuine and worthy of him; and on the other hand his heart is troubled and uncertain until he sees to some extent the Being before whom he lays his offering and to whom he entrusts it.

14. The animal man indeed prays to God, but he knows not how to pray as he should.[35] He asks something of God apart from himself or what leads to him—great prosperity in his station in life and outstanding prudence in his day,[36] but not a conscience innocent of evil deeds and a heart pure of perverse thoughts. He offers himself to God such as he is, desiring and seeking undoubtedly something apart from God. And he seeks only a God like unto himself, one who gives what he is asked, but not himself. If at any time he seems to direct his thoughts to him to whom he prays, he is satisfied, as if with the eyes of his heart[37] fast shut, to propose God to himself, and think of him as unthinkable, invisible and incomprehensible. It does not satisfy him to think of God or look upward to him as he is; he cares only that he has the power to grant what is asked for. This man sometimes prays with the spirit, but not with the understanding. His spirit, that is, his will, prays, but his understanding is unfruitful.[38] When we give our attention to God, we never do so unfruitfully, even when we ask, but reasonably, for something other than himself. But this man, multiplying words in his prayer[39] sometimes without comprehension, thoughts without understanding, does not seek comprehension of God or affection for him. Even if these should present themselves to him as it were spontaneously, he turns them into something else. For him therefore, as of old for Israel according to the flesh, the God to whom he prays is ever in the dark cloud.[40]

15. This manner of prayer finds no acceptance in the song of love. The Bride, who knows but one desire and one love, fixes upon one

---

35. Cf. Rom 8:26; 1 Cor 2:14.
37. Cf. Eph 1:18.
39. Cf. Mt 6:7.

36. Cf. Lk 16:8.
38. Cf. 1 Cor 14:14f.
40. Cf. Ex 24:16.

petition and one prayer. A sort of "animal prayer" may indeed be seen in the saints, when they sometimes ask for things that also please the workers of iniquity, such as temporal peace, fertility of the earth and health of body. But this kind of prayer does not mean that they join in the excesses of the wicked; even though they ask for something apart from God, they have no motive or end in view save himself. They offer their petition piously and devoutly, and they entrust and wholly abandon to God's will the granting or withholding of the object of their prayer.

16. Sometimes he who is in this state sets before the eyes of his understanding our Lord and Savior in his human form. As man would deal with man, he clothes his prayer with a certain human and, so to speak, bodily affection, placing on the one side him to whom he prays, on the other himself who prays, and in the midst, as it were, the thing for which he prays. To this arrangement he conforms the manner of his prayer.

Ordinarily this manner of praying is more apt to be that of a religious who, in his simplicity, does not yet perceive the things that are of God, than that of a person swayed by idle sensuality or human prudence. The simple man faithfully lays down what he has in the presence of Jesus the kindly Judge and settles himself at his feet, spiritually washing them with tears and anointing them with the ointment of godly devotion.[41] Imagining these things in a rather bodily manner, he often deserves to be enlightened by the sweetness of this sensual imagination and to grow in ardent affection for spiritual prayer and contemplation. From these bodily imaginings, he arrives—without knowing how—at understanding certain mysteries of piety. This comes to pass in the simple heart far more by God-given grace than by the effort of the one who prays. For he loves much, and therefore much is granted or forgiven him;[42] and even in matters which are exterior, he often deserves to obtain much.

41. Cf. Lk 7:38.   42. *Ibid.*

17. Certainly it is devout to draw near to God even in this way; and, as Job says, by thus visiting his beauty in God—that is, thinking of his likeness to God—a man shall not sin.[43] The Lord God of all is to be adored and worshipped beneath the mask of many faces. But nevertheless, to this very day, Jesus says to his disciples, "It is expedient for you that I depart," that is, that I withdraw the mask of my humanity from your sight, "for if I do not go, the Advocate will not come to you."[44] For as long as he who prays thinks of anything bodily in him to whom he prays, his prayer is indeed devout, but not entirely spiritual. "God is spirit," and it is needful that he who adores him should adore him in spirit and in truth.[45]

18. This manner of prayer is ordinarily drawn from the formulary of faith, the creed. Through the devotion of Christian faith, what is faithfully believed is loved in truth and simplicity, and the mental image of the outward events of the economy of our salvation in the Lord Jesus Christ is transformed into love.

19. Therefore the rational man who is led by reason, under reason's guidance in this respect, labors and strives laboriously until, victor over himself, he rises above all mental pictures and makes his escape into the realm of spiritual things. His good will is transformed into good intelligence, and the desire with which he has been tending godward is replaced by understanding and love; for now he sees, now he has fruition of God. The Holy Spirit helps this man's infirmity.[46] Then his beauty begins to be renewed in the image of God. Grace, supervening, forms his reason and understanding, his life, manners and physical temperament even, into a single affection of godliness, a single image of charity, a single face—the face of one who seeks God. This man then aspires to know God insofar as is lawful, and to be known by him. He desires that the face of his grace may be revealed to him, and that God himself may be revealed to his conscience, so that knowing him

43. Cf. Job 5:24.   44. Jn 16:7.
45. Cf. Jn 4:24.   46. Cf. Rom 8:26.

and being known by him, he may pray to him and adore him as he must in spirit and truth.

20. Here then we have the Bridegroom and the Bride, and here we have their mutual conversation. For when, according to the Lord's promise,[47] God in his divine greatness begins to come to him who loves him and make his abode with him, he becomes known to him in a certain measure. Now man cannot see God's face and live,[48] cannot, that is, attain in this life full knowledge of him. God then, in his divine greatness, places in the understanding of his lover and entrusts to him a certain quasi-knowledge of himself—consisting not in an imaginary phantasm, but in a certain devout affection, which a man yet living in the flesh is able to grasp and endure. This is the first fruit of the Spirit, the pledge and dowry of the bridal chamber, and it is nobler and richer in proportion as the Bride is readier for the Bridegroom's chamber or nearer to it.

21. When a man of desires[49] has received from God this quasi-knowledge, he confides it not so much to his own control, in his memory, as to the grace of God in his conscience. When he comes back to prayer, he will call it forth again. Then he will offer his Creator both his petition and the grace received as pledge, and thus he will appear before him with greater confidence. The more often he returns this quasi-knowledge to its source, and the more devoutly and faithfully he gives it back, the more it becomes worthy of God and effectual and sweet to its possessor.

This is indeed the ordinary procedure in the acquisition of ordinary knowledge, whatever its object, that an image of the thing known is impressed on the mind or memory, and the thing known is better known in proportion as one has within oneself a clearer image of it. But when it is a question of man's knowledge of God, the soul may sometimes find impressed upon itself a certain great resemblance to the Divinity known in one way or another. This takes place in the soul without any phantasm of the imagination.

47. Cf. Jn 14:23.   48. Cf. Ex 33:20.   49. Cf. Dan 9:23; 10:11.

It is brought about by the purity of a direct tending toward God and by the sense of enlightened love. In the common knowledge of things, the imagination of them seems to accomplish this in the memory of the knower. But the sublimity of the divine nature causes a vast unlikeness between the image impressed in the mind and the Reality, because the likeness becomes inferior inasmuch as it is in an inferior nature, and more unlike inasmuch as it is in an unlike substance—that is, the likeness of the Creator in the creature and of God in the soul.

But again, that grace of the knowledge of God, which, as has been said, is not given except in the sense or understanding of enlightened love, above every sort of knowledge of created things, of itself enriches and beatifies him who knows it. It comes down to him and lifts him up to itself. It changes for him the splendors of its sublime origin into intimate and loving affections and experiences of a certain divine sweetness and goodness. Grace does this for that blessed man who is poor in spirit,[50] humble, quiet, trembling at the Lord's words,[51] simple of soul and accustomed to the Holy Spirit's communication. And it does it the more sweetly when he truly and devoutly recognizes how he failed in poverty, humility and simplicity before he was dignified by this knowledge and understanding; and when he applies thereto his faculties, made keener by simplicity, relying less on book learning than on the powers of the Lord and his justice alone.[52]

22. This is the white pebble of the Apocalypse, bearing written upon it a name which no man knows but he that receives it.[53] This is the sweetness of which we read (among the praises of Wisdom): "Neither is it found in the land of them that live in delights."[54] This man of prayer then, be he rational or spiritual (he is rational insofar as he is guided to his goal by reason, and spiritual in the measure of his attainment once he has attained it), has in his soul,

50. Cf. Mt 5:3.   51. Cf. Is 66:2.   52. Cf. Mt 6:33.
53. Cf. Rev 2:17.   54. Job 28:13.

thanks to creative grace, the likeness and image of God. This resembles God's knowledge more closely the more it can seize eternal realities; and it can seize eternal realities in proportion as it is pure of the passing transitory things of this world, thanks to illuminating grace.[55] For as long as God is not seen save in a glass and in riddle, man will succeed in contemplating him only through an image. Whether it be the glass or the riddle[56] (that is, be the image clearer or more obscure), man in his lifetime will succeed in this only through an image. But in proportion as the soul has kept more faithfully within it the dignity and truth of God's image, it ascends toward God by means of images that are more faithful and closer to the truth. The soul must take care not to imagine in God, or with regard to God, by fanciful or superstitious presumption, what is not in itself; but by the power and facility this form of affection gives, it must draw near to him who is.[57]

23. In this life, however, to promise or to hope for the perfection of the vision or knowledge of God is the height of vain presumption. The man of whom we speak prays to God as God; reason so counsels him, spiritual progress teaches him this, and affection forms him for it. He does not conform God to himself but himself to God. He asks of God nothing but himself and the means of attaining him.[58] He is satisfied to enjoy nothing but him, or in him, and even to nothing save to attain him. While this man is working out his purification, he is rational; but when he is purified, he is spiritual. But as the rational state should always progress toward the spiritual,

55. William likes to speak of the different kinds of grace; attracting, beatifying, creating, operating, etc. (cf. Analytic Index, *infra*), but his favorite expression and reality is that of illuminating grace. The expression is found also in his other writings, e.g. *Mirror of Faith* (PL 180: 373, 376, 386, 391; trans. G. Webb and A. Walker, pp. 26, 32, 47, 52), *On Contemplating God*, no. 3. It refers especially to the graces of mystical or infused contemplation.

56. Cf. 1 Cor 13:12.

57. Cf. Ex 3:14; Heb 11:6.

58. We have here a beautiful example of the consciseness of William's Latin: *Nihil petet ab eo nisi ipsum et ad ipsum.*

E

so the spiritual state must sometimes revert to the rational. That a spiritual man should always act spiritually is something never to be attained in this life; nevertheless the man of God should always be either rational in what he seeks or spiritual in what he loves. Sometimes when he prays it seems to him that by dint of labor and struggle he has overcome and transcended all the obscurity caused by his troublesome imagination. But sometimes, solely by the operation of grace, the holy effort of the good will is neither impeded by imagination nor clouded by obscurity. Suddenly the attraction of love springs up unhoped for in him who prays[59] and, if fancies of imagination arise, they serve as a help rather than a hindrance. For when the eyes are very weak, an intermingling of images will not always be useless or harmful. They are a sort of vehicle offered by the body. Being accustomed to the sight and knowledge of bodies and bodily things, the spirit of him who prays or contemplates is thereby transported to the realm of truth; and although it is only an image, man's thought, by the vehicle of this image, is borne onward to the truth which attracts it.

24. Therefore the Holy Spirit, when he was about to deliver over to men the canticle of spiritual love, took the story which inwardly is all spiritual and divine and clothed it outwardly in images borrowed from the love of the flesh. Love alone fully understands divine things; therefore the love of the flesh[60] must be led along and transformed into the love of the spirit so that it may quickly comprehend things like to itself. Since it is impossible that true love, pining for truth, should long rest content with images, it very quickly passes, by a path known to itself, into that which was imagined. Even after a man becomes spiritual, he still shares in the delights of fleshly love which are natural to him; but when

59. In his *Letter to the Carthusians of Mont Dieu,* William speaks of this grace of prayer which precedes sometimes the effort to pray; cf. no. 46, trans. Shewring, p. 81.

60. The "love of the flesh" of which the author speaks here is that love of the Sacred Humanity of which he speaks in no. 16, *supra.*

they have come into the possession of the Holy Spirit, he devotes them all to the service of spiritual love. This is why, without telling her name or whence she comes or to whom she is speaking, as if brazenly bursting forth from a hiding place, the heroine proclaims: "Let him kiss me with the kiss of his mouth!"[61]

25. O Love, from whom all love, even that which is fleshly and degenerate takes its name! O Love, holy and sanctifying, pure and purifying! You, Life who are life-giving! Show us the meaning of your holy canticle, reveal the mystery of your kiss and the inner pulsing of your murmured song wherewith, to the hearts of your sons, you chant your power and the delights of your sweetness. Teach us your secret commands whereby you make yourself known to them who share your fellowship. That they may merit the capacity to receive you, you first cleanse them of the filth of things which may not be desired or delighted in by any heart wherein you deign to dwell, since you are from above and draw us heavenward, but all these things are from beneath. Teach us to enter into the place of the wonderful tabernacle, even to the house of God, with the voice of joy and praise, the glad sound of one feasting.[62] Teach us to attain the state of soul which issues in this jubilation of one who feasts, or rather of one who after the banquet finds his hunger sharper yet and cries: "Let him kiss me with the kiss of his mouth!"[63]

---

61. Song 1:1.
62. Cf. Ps 41:5.
63. Song 1:1.

FIRST SONG

PRELUDE OR ARGUMENT

IT MAY be inferred from the order of happenings which ensue and the form of the words that as of old the Egyptian princess came to Solomon,[1] so the sinful soul after her conversion came to Christ, was solemnly received as a Bride, generously dowered and brought into the storerooms where the royal wealth was kept. And there, when she had been nourished with milk from the Bridegroom's breasts and steeped in the fragrance of his perfumes, the Bridegroom's name and the mystery of that name were revealed to her. At length, as if the fire of love had been kindled in the Bride's heart, the Bridegroom suddenly went out and departed, and all the grace and glory of the storerooms vanished with him. Taking from her the presence of his grace and the joy of his countenance, he departed and hid himself from her (as the gospel says with reference to our Lord and the Jews).[2]

27. We must not disregard the fact that in the storerooms lie the reserves of our King's royal riches and delights. The use of them is sound and effective, and the enjoyment quickening. When they are eaten, they give life; when drunk, they impart joy; they nourish, and they strengthen. The entire use and enjoyment of them remain within the very being of the person who uses or enjoys them. They are not like gold and silver and other such things, the only use of which is to be seen and possessed. Some of these riches

1. Cf. 1 Kings 3:1.   2. Cf. Jn 8:59.

21

and delights are amassed in the storerooms, but others are placed only in the cellar of wine. Now a vast distance, measured not by space but by importance as to both grace and dignity, separates the storerooms from the cellar of wine. The treasures they contain are spoken of by the prophet where he says: "The riches of salvation are wisdom and knowledge."[3] The storerooms represent the fullness of knowledge; this is why they are named in the plural, since as another prophet says: "Times pass over and knowledge is made manifold."[4] For wisdom, indeed, which is denoted by the cellar of wine, only one thing is necessary. The knowledge referred to belongs to Christian godliness, not puffing up but edifying in charity.[5] In the understanding of the Scriptures and in matters of faith, behavior and life, it is well-instructed prudence. In the human soul it is the rational part, the rightful place of faith and hope, and charity too, although the cellar of wine is charity's proper habitation.

28. For as it is impossible to love God without believing in him, so anyone who truly believes in him or hopes in him or knows him cannot fail to love him. The cellar of wine is wisdom; wisdom is both piety, by which is denoted worship of God, and the uplifting of the soul from a lower to a higher level, not by pretentious knowledge but by devout love. This occurs when man's spirit raises itself to the loftiest of spiritual things so that he may know God's eternal immutability insofar as mutable men may know it, and learn his immutable reasons for the judgment of mutable things. Although these reasons are beyond man, still they are not entirely alien to the nature of human reason. This is plain because it is only thanks to them that even men who contravene them by their evil lives will sometimes make judgments that are true and right. Whatever human reason does or knows aright, derives form and knowledge from these reasons alone, for everything receives being from them and rests on them, and all things that exist return to them.

3. Is 33:6.   4. Dan 12:4.   5. Cf. 1 Cor 8:1.

As it is the part of knowledge and faith to act and understand with regard to Christ in what belongs to the dispensation of Providence regarding his human life, so it is the part of wisdom and love to taste and contemplate in him the glory of the divine majesty and, even in human things, the power of his divine operation. Where the behavior of the spiritual man is concerned, the part played by knowledge and reason in his activity belongs to wisdom in the affective order. Knowledge amasses treasures, but not for itself. Like the bees, it makes honey, but for someone else. It is allowed a certain outward use of the things it has amassed, but their inward savor is reserved for another, and for another place. The study by which knowledge is gained requires the discipline of life in society, but the perfection of wisdom calls for solitude and secrecy and a heart that is solitary even amid the crowd.

29. The Bride, therefore, once she was brought into the storerooms, learned many things about the Bridegroom and many things about herself. There all the gifts conferred upon her at her first audience with the Bridegroom—the milk of the breasts, the sweet smell of the perfumes, the revelation of the Bridegroom's name and the outpouring of his perfume—were an incitement to love and a favor from him who was drawing her. But after this, his purifying action took hold of her, that she might be trained and purified but not utterly abandoned. The Bridegroom went forth and withdrew; and thereupon she was wounded by charity, enkindled with desire of him who was absent, drawn by the charm of a holy newness, and renewed by the taste of goodness. Then suddenly she is cast aside and left to herself.[6] The very storerooms

6. In the *Mirror of Faith* (trans. G. Webb and A. Walker, pp. 68f.) there is a passage which expresses the pain of the soul that is banished from the vision to the work of making itself more clean, and at the same time its recognition of the justice of that banishment, its patience and the discipline of purgation. For the necessity of purity of soul, see also Meditation 4 and the *Letter to the Carthusians of Mont Dieu*, no. 64, trans. Shewring, p. 110. The same idea in different words is expressed *infra*, no. 157.

disgust her since they are empty and deserted; or rather, we are to understand that what disgusts her is knowledge which, in the Bridegroom's absence, brings her nothing but grief, as it is written: "He that adds knowledge, adds also grief."[7] Accompanied by the young maidens who shared with her to a certain extent in the favor received in the storerooms, she hastens away, led by the perfume of her vanished Bridegroom. And in the ardor of her desire, she gives voice to the first words of the sacred song, exclaiming, "Let him kiss me with the kiss of his mouth!"[8]

7. Eccles 1:18. William will return to this idea of knowledge causing grief (cf. *infra*, nos. 36, 122). It is a common theme in the writings of the Cistercian Fathers. Isaac of Stella develops it most deeply in his Fourth Sermon for Sexagesima.

8. Song 1:1.

Let him kiss me with the kiss of his mouth!
For your breasts are better than wine,
Smelling sweet of the best perfumes.

Your name is as oil poured out.

Therefore young maidens have loved you.
Draw me after you; we will run
Into the fragrance of your perfumes.[1]

I HAVE SEEN, says the Bride, his face shine upon me;[2] I have perceived the gladness of his countenance;[3] I have felt the grace poured abroad in his lips.[4] Let no one interfere, let no one step between; let him kiss me himself with the kiss of his mouth, for I will no longer endure, I will no longer receive the breath of a stranger's kiss. All other kisses savor ill to me; but the kiss of the Bridegroom breathes a divine fragrance.

A kiss is a certain outward loving union of bodies, sign and incentive of an inward union. It is produced by use of the mouth and aims, by mutual exchange, at a union not only of bodies but of spirits. Christ the Bridegroom offered to his Bride the Church, so to speak, a kiss from heaven, when the Word made flesh drew so near to her that he wedded her to himself; and so wedded her

1. Song 1:1ff.   2. Cf. Ps 118:135.
3. Cf. Ps 15:11.   4. Cf. Ps 44:3.

that he united her to himself, in order that God might become man, and man might become God. He also offers this same kiss to the faithful soul, his Bride, and imprints it upon her, when from the remembrance of the benefits common to all men, he gives her her own special and personal joy and pours forth within her the grace of his love, drawing her spirit to himself and infusing into her his spirit, that both may be one spirit.

31. In the storerooms, as the Bridegroom withdrew, the Bride had received this kiss from him in a partial manner and had been set on fire with eagerness to attain its perfection and full sweetness, whereof the Lord said, as he prayed to the Father for his disciples: "Father, I will that as you and I are one, so they also may be one in us, that the love wherewith you have loved me may be in them, and I in them."[5] Why, if not that she who had received of his fullness, and grace for grace[6] (that is, the grace of love for the grace of faith), now desired that very fullness—the fullness of the Holy Spirit who is the unity and the love of the Father and of the Son—and the full joy in him which no man might take from her?[7] She wished to be dissolved and to be with Christ, thinking, after a taste of the highest Good, that it was no longer needful for her to abide still in the flesh.[8]

32. If any have not learned, let them learn; let them turn around and see; let them rouse their curiosity to experience how this drama enacts itself in the behavior and the conscience of persons who, being now converted to the Lord, walk in newness of life.[9] The affection and entire life of these souls are divided between grief and joy—grief for the absence of the Bridegroom and joy at his presence; and their one hope is the eternal joy of the vision of him. And they experience this not once or in one manner, but often and in many different manners. All this laborious but holy exercise in the heart of the lover (that is, the life of the proficient) is the affair not of a single day but of considerable time; it is manifold and

5. Cf. Jn 17:21, 26. 6. Cf. Jn 1:16. 7. Cf. Jn 16:22.
8. Cf. Phil 1:23. 9. Cf. Rom 6:4.

varied, following the devotion of the soul's different attractions and the course of its spiritual progress.

33. For you, O Bridegroom of chaste souls, say to the Bride: "I go away, and I come,"[10] nor do you remain with her forever. In like manner, O Father of orphans, by the prudent counsel of your wisdom, while your children are exiled in a land not their own, you suffer them sometimes to be disheartened in the grief of their desire, as if shut out from you, and to pine away with love for your love. You purify them in the furnace of their poverty, drawing them to yourself the more strongly by the very difficulty of attaining you. But sometimes, by the sweetness of your grace, you open to your little ones of your own accord, nor do you turn them away when they reach you. You suffer them to lie down and weep in your bosom; they weep and refuse to be comforted, lest they be prevented from weeping in your presence, while they esteem as your highest gift the privilege of weeping in your bosom. For they find it exceedingly good and sweet to weep before you, O Lord their God who did create them;[11] and you form them for this very end, that they may weep in your bosom. And when you deign to wipe away the flood of their tears, they flow the more; because the very hand of him who wipes away these tears, sweetly causes them a certain grief which attracts and soothes them; and the harder they weep, the more greatly it consoles them by the conviction of good hope. For that stream of tears gives them such joy that it clearly manifests your presence;[12] yet at the same time your children, sojourning in a strange land, cannot forget that they are pilgrims.[13] That joy and that grief, while they exist together, call forth sweet and delightful tears; tears, because of grief; sweet, because of love, love of you, O Love. To suffer before you is great joy; to weep before you, supreme consolation;[14] and to rejoice in you is supreme beatitude.

10. Jn 14:28. 11. Cf. Ps 94:6. 12. Cf. Ps 45:5.
13. Cf. Ps 136:4. 14. Cf. Mt 5:4.

34. All this sweetness of him who consoles and of her who grieves, of him who attracts and of her who runs, of him who caresses and of her who loves, of him who speaks and of her who answers, permeates the words and events of this Song from end to end. But the action always takes place in the conscience and heart of the Bride, whoever she is, as she pours out her soul before the Lord her God and hears with joy what the Lord God speaks in her. The familiar conversation of Bridegroom and Bride is both the witness and the devotion of a well-disposed conscience. In the Bride's conscience the Bridegroom bears witness to her merit; and the Bride's devotion, rich in gratitude, renders to the Bridegroom the dutiful love which she owes him.

35. The Bride, therefore, has gone forth from the King's storerooms, into which she had been brought that she might contemplate the lovely things of the Bridegroom; and she has left the taste and pleasant experience of those good things. Now she desires only the one who is himself lovable, whom his lovely things commend; for she has received the pledge of the Spirit, and she faints after God's salvation. I am weary, she says, of these storerooms, empty because of the Bridegroom's absence; I am weary of these daily repeated promises, these obscure secrets, these parables and proverbs, the glass and the riddle.[15] I desire the mystery of the kingdom of God; I entreat that the Father may be spoken to me plainly[16]—face to face,[17] eye to eye,

Cf. p. 21 or 29.   15. Cf. 1 Cor 13:12.   16. Cf. Jn 16:25

17. 1 Cor 13:12. William frequently alludes to this text (*infra*, nos. 36, 152, 176, 183). For him the spiritual life might be defined as "seeking the face of God." He is devoted to the texts of Scripture which speak of the face of God, e.g. Gen 32:30: "I have seen the Lord face to face and my soul has been saved;" Ps 26:8 (in the alternate version): "I have sought your face, your face I have sought, O Lord;" Ps 23:6: "This is the generation seeking him, seeking the face of the God of Jacob" (see e.g. *Letter to the Carthusians of Mont Dieu*, no. 8, trans. Shewring, pp. 18f.). He lived before the face of God, and from "the light of his countenance" (cf. *infra*, nos. 43, 59, 67) came the graces of contemplation. He was convinced that God aids with his countenance him who looks at him. He moves him and excites him. The beauty of the sovereign good

kiss to kiss: "Let him kiss me with the kiss of his mouth!"[18]

36. But why does she say, "Let him kiss me," as if he were absent, and not rather, "Kiss me"? It seems that in the storerooms she had striven much to see him face to face and as he is, and to know him even as she was known by him[19]—which is the kiss of perfection. And it seems that the Bridegroom, by the agency of the prophets, apostles and other doctors, by the knowledge of the Scriptures, had offered her, so to speak, sundry kisses of his grace; then, as though satisfaction had been given her, he withdrew and departed. She at once began to complain, as one chides the absent, impatiently calling after him and crying: "Let him kiss me with the kiss of his mouth!" Just as if she said: How long must I put up with these alien kisses of knowledge that adds to my sorrow? Even though I deserve not that kiss of perfection or any other, before he withdraws from me, let him grant me the kiss of his mouth. A kiss that is passed on is, indeed, good; but it seems not to retain the full strength of its charm when it is transferred from vessel to vessel. What his ministers bring gives knowledge; but what the breath of his mouth and of his kiss inspires, gives savor; and it will give full savor when my joy in him shall be full.

37. While he withdraws, she follows him with her gaze until he is out of sight; and finding it sweet to address him even though he no longer hears, she says: "For your breasts are better than wine!"[20] As if she had been interrogated whence came such hasty presumption and such a confident request for this kiss, she says: "From the breasts, O Lord, of your consolation,"[21] "for your breasts are better than wine"—sweeter to suck, more potent to give joy, quicker to

---

draws him who contemplates him. He expressed his life's aspirations in the words of Ps 30:21: "Hide me, I beg you, in the hidden places of your face . . ." Cf. *On the Nature and Dignity of Love,* ch. 9, trans. G. Webb and A. Walker, p. 45; also Meditation 4 and *Letter to the Carthusians of Mont Dieu,* no. 3, trans. Shewring, pp. 11f.

18. Song 1:1.	19. Cf. 1 Cor 13:12.
20. Song 1:1.	21. Cf. Is 66:11.

cause inebriation. Because they have nourished me, I desire the kiss; because they have inebriated me, I presume to it.

38. For as long as man lives and labors here, many are the charismatic gifts,[22] many the different kinds of consolation given to the children of grace, in the distribution of graces, the forward march of progress or the success of virtues. And in all this, in the splendors of divine illumination, in the outbursts of devout compunction, in the ecstasies of divine contemplation, it is your breasts, O eternal Wisdom, that nourish the holy infancy of your little ones and bear witness that your presence will not be wanting to them until the consummation of the world.[23] But when their time comes, the time appointed by your good pleasure, may their mouths never be accounted unworthy to kiss your mouth in the fullness of your perfect knowledge, since in the time of their patience and endurance you offered them, by means of these breasts, your own milk to nourish spiritual knowledge and speed progress toward your perfection! For if they have ever sucked elsewhere anything poisonous, they must needs be healed and cleansed by contact with these sacred breasts and the power and fragrance of your healthful perfumes. Since that everlasting blessed union and the kiss of eternity are denied the Bride on account of her human condition and weakness, she turns to your bosom; and not attaining to that mouth of yours, she puts her mouth to your breasts instead, and rests there saying: "For your breasts are better than wine!"

39. And at the same time, mark well that in the petition for the kiss, the highest affection in prayer possible to a human being has directed the Bride's gaze toward that light of God's countenance; but dazzled by the brilliancy of his charity, before long she turns back to the more common practices of the spiritual life and applies

22. William employs the term "charismatic gifts" here in a broader sense than the later theologians who follow St Paul. He (cf. 1 Cor 12) spoke of the charisms as gifts which were given to the individual primarily "for the common good."

23. Cf. Mt 28:20.

herself thereto when she says: "For your breasts are better than wine, smelling sweet of the best perfumes. Your name is as oil poured out."[24] No sooner did I come to you, she says, than you laid bare to me the breasts of your sweetness, the first nourishment of your grace. Through the sweetness of your suavity and the good felt by conscience, they are better than any wine of worldly wisdom or joy of fleshly pleasure; they exhale the fragrance of the best ointments, which are the gifts of the sevenfold Spirit.[25] For when, by your operation, those same gifts were given me in their order, your fear first of all laid hold of me, impelling me sternly toward you. In the second place piety met me, sweetly receiving me in you. This, as it is written, is your worship, for Job says: "Piety is the worship of God,"[26] since it teaches me to worship you. It has taught me to say in the Holy Spirit: "The Lord Jesus!"[27]

And soon, in the odor of sweetness and the power of health, the oil of this same name of yours is poured out from you and poured into me, softening all my rigidity, smoothing all roughness and healing my infirmities. Before the oil of your name, the yoke of my former captivity turns to dust, but your yoke, O Lord, becomes sweet to me and your burden light.[28] For the sound of your name— "Lord," "Jesus" or "Christ"—straightway gives to my hearing joy and gladness,[29] because as soon as your name sounds in the ears, the mystery of your name also shines forth in the heart and your love in the affections. Then it calls forth devout service of the Lord, affection and love of the Savior (which is the meaning of "Jesus"), and obedience and fear of Christ the King.

---

24. Song 1:1f.   25. Cf. Is 11:3.

26. Job 28:28 (*Septuagint*). William expresses his notion of worshipful piety more fully in his *Letter to the Carthusians of Mont Dieu,* no. 9: "For this piety is the perpetual mindfulness of God, the continual striving of the will for the understanding of him, the unwearied affection for love of him. . . ." The whole of no. 9 should be read: Shewring, pp. 20f.

27. 1 Cor 12:3.   28. Cf. Mt 11:30.   29. Cf. Ps 50:10.

40. For it is just, O Lord Jesus, that at every name of yours every knee should bend of those in heaven, on earth and under the earth,[30] because you are called by no name that has not some relation to us. And there is not one of these relations, signified by one or other of your names, but implies your goodness towards us. For as "Lord" you lord it over us by doing good; as "Jesus" you save us; as "Christ," that is, "anointed" Priest and King, you reign over us and intercede for us. For this relation of Son to the Father, whereby you were predestined and were made the Son of God in power,[31] is known by those who have learned to cry in the Holy Spirit: "Abba, Father!"[32] And they understand that by this they are made sons of God and your brethren, and the outpouring of oil is given and apportioned to us. It is in this that you have redeemed us, O good Brother—and had you not redeemed us, neither man nor angel nor any created being would redeem us. Coming as the only Son, you did not will to remain alone but brought into glory many sons whom you were not ashamed to call brethren, saying: "I will declare your name to my brethren."[33]

41. Therefore, says the Bride, because of the sweetness of your breasts and the healthfulness of your name, like unto oil, the young maidens, with me, have also loved you. They are young plants[34] set out for your service, young souls renewed in the spirit of their mind,[35] walking in newness of spirit,[36] ascending in their heart step by step and going from virtue to virtue,[37] progressing from glory to glory as through the Spirit of the Lord.[38] Each of them exclaims: "Draw me after you!"[39] And then they say in chorus: "We will run into the fragrance of your perfumes!"[40]

---

30. Cf. Phil 2:10.   31. Cf. Rom 1:4.   32. Rom 8:15; Gal. 4:6.

33. Heb 2:12; William's consideration here of the Holy Name finds a close affinity to that of St Bernard in the latter's Fifteenth Sermon on the Song of Songs.

34. Cf. Ps 143:12.   35. Cf. Eph 4:23.   36. Cf. Rom 6:4.

37. Cf. Ps 83:6, 8.   38. Cf. 2 Cor 3:18.   39. Song 1:3.

40. *Ibid.*

42. The fragrance of perfumes is the fame of the Bridegroom's virtues, found fragrant by the young maidens who are progressing: the force that draws them is the incitement of charity. Indeed the unction which teaches the Bride concerning all things abides.[41] And there is a great distance between that fragrance and this unction. Yet being excluded from the storerooms and deserted by the Bridegroom, she is now of almost equal condition with the young maidens, since she is fed by nothing but the fragrance of the Bridegroom. Therefore she too seems to say with them: "We will run into the fragrance of your perfumes!" But when she is drawn, she runs, for she wishes to be incited; and while the charm of the fragrance instills in her the power of the unction, there is no delay, no difficulty in the course of her spiritual progress. As he flees, she pursues him, proclaiming and recalling his favors to her—his breasts and his perfumes, the fragrance and the oil poured out. For the grateful remembrance of past favors is a wise and excellent kind of prayer, pleasing to God and effectual for the securing of yet other gifts.

43. "Draw me after you," says the Bride, "we will run into the fragrance of your perfumes!" Behold her now weary and ready to faint, and needing to be drawn—unless the fragrance of him whom she no longer sees still draws her and leads her to run. This is why she says: "We will run into the fragrance of your perfumes!" As if she said: even though at the present moment I am not deserving of the joy of your countenance or the kiss of your mouth, at least do not withdraw from me the fragrance of your perfumes. For the presence of the Bridegroom is memory well-disposed toward him; it is intelligence enlightened by the light of his countenance;[42] and it is the unction of the Holy Spirit teaching the soul concerning all things.[43] The fragrance of perfumes which vanish with him is a certain impression, still living in the memory, of vanished sweetness

---

41. That is, the gifts of the Holy Spirit; cf. no. 39, *supra*.

42. Cf. Ps 88:16.

43. Cf. Jn 14:26.

F

and, in what thought still recaptures, the joy of dwelling on the remembrance of consolation once possessed. "So we will run," she says, "into the fragrance of your perfumes"; if this perfume continues and draws us, we will continue to run; but if it ceases, we must also cease. For this reason, making memory of favors received, she adds these words; "The King has brought me into his storerooms."[44]

44. Song 1:3.

STANZA 2

The King has brought me into his storerooms.

We will be glad and rejoice in you,
Remembering your breasts more than wine.

The righteous love you.[1]

FIRST the Bride takes pleasure in giving the title of King to him she would fain have reign over her; just as one who loves to serve him, expressing his mind and will by speech, says in the Holy Spirit: "The Lord Jesus!"[2] Then straightway she conceives a vaster hope; and from this hope, she kindles again a greater love for him who has vanished. Thereupon, as if she were once more fixing her eyes upon him, she says: "We will be glad and rejoice in you, remembering your breasts" whose milk has fed me, whose perfumes have anointed me, whose fragrance has strengthened me.

See what efforts she makes, how anxious she is. One minute she speaks *to* him; the next she speaks *of* him. A lover is never content with merely one way of reaching the object of his love. Therefore she sighs more eagerly than ever to contemplate him who is not present and says: "The righteous love you!"

45. All animals are naturally bent over towards their belly and the earth. Man alone, with his body upright, stands erect, lifting himself heavenward. In this way nature manifests that he has some-

1. Song 1:3.   2. 1 Cor 12:3.

35

thing in common with the inhabitants of heaven. Therefore the
Bride says, "The righteous love you," the righteous being the
upright, in other words, men; for anyone who is not upright
through love for you, is no man but a beast.

46. We must not pass over the three points put forward here
with regard to the King's storerooms but weigh and analyze them
in detail: the memory of benefits received, the hope of benefits to
come and, for both, uprightness of love in thanksgiving. "We will
be glad and rejoice in you," she says, and this is for the future. Of
the past: "Remembering your breasts." And the third thing is:
"The righteous love you." By the memory of things past, we cling
to the Lord our God;[3] hope for the future restrains us from wishing
to withdraw from him; and upright love so strengthens us that we
cannot forsake him.

But in the Bridegroom's absence, the remembrance of the storerooms warns the children of the Bridegroom to take refuge in the
comfort of the Scriptures[4] when they are deprived of the grace of
spiritual consolation. For as she who is a Bride, when she is transported in mind to God, following the Lamb wherever he goes,[5]
offers her entire self in love; so once she becomes sober, returning
to herself,[6] she must recollect her entire being in understanding
and nourish her soul at leisure with the fruit of spiritual knowledge,
she must return to the memory of the storerooms and the breasts
of the Bridegroom. That is, as has been said, she must take refuge
in the comfort of the Scriptures. The two Testaments are for her
the two breasts of the Bridegroom. From them is to be sucked the
milk of all the mysteries accomplished in time for our eternal
salvation, in order to attain to the food which is theWord of God,
God with God.[7] For Christ, in his humility, is our milk; God,
equal with God, he is our food.[8] Milk nourishes, and food brings
about growth. But it is in the storerooms that these breasts are

---

3. Cf. Duet 4:4.   4. Cf. Rom 15:4.   5. Cf. Rev 14:4.
6. Cf. 2 Cor 5:13.   7. Cf. Jn 1:1f.   8. Cf. Jn 6:56.

given in suck, because these mysteries are understood in the Scriptures. The Bride sucked at the breasts when she first understood; she remembers the breasts when she meditates on what she has understood. Here she finds exultation for her body and joy for her soul; for after corruption her body is promised incorruption,[9] and her soul is promised the vision of God; and in the love of God, her uprightness is duly ordered.

9. Cf. 1 Cor 15:42, 53.

I am black but beautiful,
   O you daughters of Jerusalem,
As the tents of Cedar,
   as the curtains of Solomon.

Look not at me, for that I am darkened;
Because the sun has altered my color.
The sons of my mother have fought against me,
They have set me as keeper in the vineyards:
My vineyards I have not kept.[1]

WHEN the sun vanishes, night must needs ensue. And when the Bridegroom vanishes and prolongs his absence, the Bride begins to lose her former beauty and turn black, and all her deeds are divested of their charm, with the result that now the former warmth is gone from her heart and the color from her deeds.[2] For just as daylight is, so to speak, the ruler over all colors, being indispensable to their beauty and strength, so illuminating grace is the strength of all the virtues and the light of all good deeds, being indispensable to their effectiveness and success. Even if they appear to attain success, this is merely illusory since they give no

---

1. Song 1:4f.

2. Here we have an example of William's balanced use of words: *nec calor sit in corde, nec color in opere.*

joy and lack the oil of gladness,[3] the unction that teaches, the taste of divine sweetness, the perfume of eternity and the powerful experience of the spiritual senses.

48. The Bride, therefore, blushing for herself and anxious about the maidens who were wont to imitate and admire her, cries out: "I am black but beautiful, O you daughters of Jerusalem, as the tents of Cedar, as the curtains of Solomon." These tents and curtains would seem to be intended for usefulness rather than beauty; it is as if she said: My beauty remains untouched, even if my color is altered, for the spirit indeed is willing, but the flesh is weak.[4] My faith is firm, but my understanding is darkened; my will is the same, but my affection has grown weak. She admits that she is black because of the obscurity of her troubled conscience; but she does not disavow that she is beautiful because of the uprightness of her faith. Since she has been nourished in the King's storerooms, she knows that to deny her faith would be not humility but impiety. For to lack not only faith but hope and good will too, is death; but to have them and deny them is a heinous offence. Indeed the Bride always finds herself beautiful on account of the upright beauty of her faith, the purity of her intention and the zeal of her will—as long as she never ceases to be a Bride and never disavows her bridehood. Sometimes, however, because of the awareness of her past sins, the assault of vices or the blindness of human ignorance, she may humbly confess her blackness.

49. "As the tents of Cedar, as the curtains of Solomon." Cedar means "darkness."[5] By this word the Bride refers to darkness of conscience or benighted reason. By the words tents and curtains, that is, portable tents shaped out of skins, she refers to instability of mind. It is obvious what a hindrance tents and curtains are to contemplation of the interior light. They belong, however, to

---

3. Cf. Ps 44:8. 4. Cf. Mt 26:41.

5. St Bernard interperts "cedar" in the same way in his Twenty-sixth Sermon on the Song of Songs.

Solomon, the true man of peace, for they are of service to the army of the brethren and the peace of the Church.

50. But tender charity is ever watchful lest it vex anyone by ill-conceived humility; or, again, lest its avowal of guilt and weakness become an example or occasion leading to a brother's downfall. Therefore the Bride continues thus: "Look not at me, for that I am darkened, because the sun has altered my color." I am not darkened enough to have grown blind, as if I lacked the eyes of reason. But the Sun of Justice[6] has withdrawn from me the light of his grace, without which eyes open in vain, colors cannot exist and all warm things turn cold. I was, she says, a coal that laid waste;[7] but now I am myself laid waste.[8] While I was in the fire, I glowed, giving off heat and light; but when the fire disappeared, I was left all black. Nevertheless my beauty remains ever untouched. Take my beauty as your pattern; although it is discolored, it has not lost all its warmth; for even if the embellishments of love have disappeared from me, its reality remains.

51. Wonder not, therefore, that in the absence of the Bridegroom I have become the prey of all and sundry. "For the sons of my mother have fought against me." How? "They have set me as keeper in the vineyards: my vineyard I have not kept." Ordinarily in the Scriptures, by wine, which cheers the heart of man,[9] is to be understood joy. For as the vineyard is the mother of wine, worldly peace is the mother of worldly joy; but spiritual peace is the mother of spiritual joy. Thus the sons of my mother, that is, the original concupiscences of human nature, fighting against me, awakened in me the desire to rule over men. Or again, the sons of my mother the Church took me away from myself, set me to rule over them and, to nourish their fleshly joys, set me as guardian of their outward peace. I am busy watching over it; and in the

---

6. Cf. Mal 4:2.   7. Cf. Ps 119:4.

8. Another play on words: *in quid fui desolatorius; nunc autem desolatus.*

9. Cf. Ps 103:15.

meantime I am becoming neglectful of my own inward joys, neglecting my inward peace. Thus the sun has altered my color, while the responsibility for fraternal charity with its dark cloud of preoccupations obscures within me the splendor of inward purity.[10]

52. What we must understand is this. While the Bride is led from one place to another, taught and instructed by various temptations, she must needs be burdened with the office of superior. In this charge she is divided among many things and finds herself insufficient for each of them in particular. Attending more anxiously to the progress of others, she herself fails to progress; and she is troubled in conscience over the harm to herself.[11] Behold her left to herself, doubtful and wavering. She wishes to pray, but she is not equal to it; she wishes to meditate, but she fails. When the Bridegroom is present, she addresses him as if he were absent; and

10. William, who long carried the burden of the abbatial office, was very conscious of how such responsibilities impeded one's freedom for divine contemplation. He spoke of it in his treatise on the *Nature and Dignity of Love* (trans. Webb and Walker, ch. 8, pp. 38f.) and in Meditation 11. It is this which led him finally to lay down his abbatial charge in 1135 and to enter the Cistercian monastery of Signy. St Bernard, too, was sensitive to this struggle that a superior had to face between the call of duty and the allurement of contemplation, as is evident from his Fifty-second and Fifty-third Sermons on the Song of Songs. Yet, when William sought his advice in regard to his resigning his abbatial office, Bernard gave him the advice: "If I am to say what I think, I must tell you that unless I am mistaken this is something I could not advise you to attempt . . . Indeed I wish for you what has for long been no secret to me that you wish for yourself. But putting aside what both of us wish, as it is right we should, it is safer for me and more advantageous for you if I advise you as I think God wishes. Therefore, I say, hold on to what you have, remain where you are, and try to benefit those over whom you rule. Do not try to escape the responsibility of your office while you are still able to discharge it for the benefit of your subjects."—Letter 86; trans. B. James, *The Letters of St Bernard of Clairvaux* (London: Burns & Oates, 1953), Letter 88, p. 128.

11. In his Thirtieth Sermon on the Song of Songs St Bernard gives voice to the same complaint of having to be neglectful of himself while fulfilling the office of superior; but then he goes on to give another possible interpretation, that of good forgetfulness of self when one goes out of oneself in love.

when he is absent, as if he were present. Nevertheless, because she is a pupil of the royal storerooms, she does not neglect the advice given by the Apostle: "Confess your sins to one another."[12] In the tribulations caused by her temptations, with never a blush at the courage of her avowal, she does not hesitate to reveal to her companions the secret faults of her conscience, when she says: "I am black but beautiful, O you daughters of Jerusalem!" And after this confession she returns with greater ardor to prayer and exclaims: "Show me, O you whom my soul loves, where you feed, where you have your couch in the midday."[13]

12. Jas 5:16. 13. Song 1:6.

STANZA 4

Show me, O you, whom my soul loves,
Where you feed,
    where you have your couch in the midday;
Lest I begin to wander
After the flocks of your companions.[1]

BEHOLD this most manifest grace: after the avowal of her faults the Bride comes to prayer, and all of a sudden she deserves to find the Bridegroom whom she seeks. With the full embrace of charity, she draws him into her heart. Presenting her lips, as it were, for his kiss, she cries: "You whom my soul loves!" For according to the historical sense, the Bridegroom has offered himself to the Bride who loves and seeks him, but he still feigns to turn away from her and wrest himself from her hands. He proves her in the secret place of tempest, in the kiss of contradiction.[2] But she approaches him with burning love and says: "O you, whom my soul loves!" And these words show first of all that, as she prays, the Holy Spirit is now helping her weakness,[3] for the Holy Spirit is that very love referred to by the Bride when she says: "O you, whom my soul loves!"

54. These are her words: "You, whom my soul loves." The soul is indeed nearly the whole man. The body is his least part. Therefore, Lord Jesus, when the soul of your Bride loves you, neglecting

1. Song 1:6.   2. Cf. Ps 80:8.   3. Cf. Rom 8:16.

and, as it were, already casting off her body, she follows you with
her whole self.[4] For your sake she desires to be put to death all the
day long;[5] she loves to lose herself in this world, so that in eternal
life she may possess herself in you.[6] Surely no doubt is possible:
she has known the hour when the face of your beauty shone upon
her, since she loves you thus; she has felt the breath of your mouth,
since she sighs for you thus; she has experienced the sweetness of
your embraces, since she abandons herself so intimately in you.
For she loves you, and she loves you only through yourself who are
the very love wherewith she loves you; and she loves you in her
soul only insofar as she loves herself in no one save in you. For if she
loves the beautiful, you are the beauty of all that is beautiful. If she
loves the good, you are the goodness of all that is good. If she loves
what is useful, every man—even one who hates—makes use of you,
while everyone who loves enjoys you.

55. Then says the Bride: "Show me, O you whom my soul
loves, where you feed, where you have your couch in the midday."
Observe how far she is borne along by the force and humility of
her confession—to a point to which the sublimity of her contemplation could not aspire when earlier she asked for the Bridegroom's
kiss and prepared herself to receive it. But now she would fain

---

4. The Cistercians come back frequently to the Augustinian and indeed the
Pauline notion of a certain struggle between body and soul; see e.g. St
Bernard's *Sermons on the Song of Songs*, Sermons 25,26,29, 30. However, they
are far from accepting any Manichean notion that the body being matter is
therefore evil. Cf. *Infra*, no. 128, where William speaks of the order of charity.
He makes it clear that there is to be love and care for the body. In his book *On
Precepts and Dispensations*, St Bernard, using the saying of the wise man—"the
corruptible body weighs down the soul" (Wis 9:15)—makes the important
distinction: "note well that this is said of the 'corruptible body' rather than
simply of the body since it is the corruption which constitutes the burden . . . .
Weighed down then not with the companionship, but rather with the infirmi-
ties of this body, we wish to be dissolved and be with Christ."—trans. C.
Greenia, *Monastic Obligations and Abbatial Authority: St Bernard's Book On
Precepts and Dispensations*, no. 59, in *The Works of Bernard of Clairvaux*, vol. 1
Cistercian Fathers Series 1). Cf. also, Isaac of Stella, Sermon 8 for Sexagesima.

5. Cf. Ps 43:22; Rom 8:36.   6. Cf. Mt 10:39.

rest in Jesus's bosom, like the beloved disciple[7] who once rested there and perceived the supreme Beginning, and in the Beginning the Word, and the Word with God.[8] "Show me," she says, that is, speak within my heart,[9] tell me what I long to ask, and let me feel it in myself by the perception of a reliable experience. Breathe upon me and let me know it experimentally through awareness of delight in you. Now what I long to ask is this: What kind of life, what state of soul, what habit of mind, what gift of grace, in the affections of him whom you render worthy, whom you turn to your purpose, you who have mercy on whom you have mercy[10]— there being question not of him who wills or him who runs, but of yourself who show mercy.[11] This is your purpose—to feed the lover's understanding with the knowledge of your truth, out of the abundance of your sweetness, and to consecrate unto yourself his memory, in which you ever have your couch with delight; showing yourself for him the noontide heat of burning love and likewise its cooling, the splendor of noontide light and likewise its shady bower.

56. Or, take this interpretation: The Bride, in the tribulation of her exertions, asks that her end be disclosed to her so that she may know what is wanting to her.[12] Seeking comfort against her inconstancy, she prays for the revelation of the day of eternity—not the day that begins with morning and ends at evening, but the one that remains forever in the noontide of warmth and light, wisdom and understanding, love and blessed fruition. On this day it is granted to the people of God to keep the great Sabbath,[13] that they may lie down and rest from all their works as God did from his.[14] It is the day whereon, in eternal beatitude, God feeds with himself

---

7. Cf. Jn 13:23.   8. Cf. Jn 1:1.

9. William's interpretation here stands out more strikingly in the Latin, where he interprets the *indica* as meaning *intus . . . dic.*

10. Cf. Ex 33:19.   11. Cf. Rom 9:15f.   12. Cf. Ps 38:5.

13. *Sabbatismus*; this expression is found also in St Augustine (*De Civitate Dei*, 22:30, trans. Marcus Dods, The Modern Library ed. [New York: Random House, 1950], p. 866) and in St Jerome (Epistle 140, no. 8).

14. Cf. Heb 4:9f.

both angels and saints; they are ever satisfied by the perfection of happiness, and ever desirous of contemplating him because of the devotion and sweetness of love.

57. Or, take this interpretation: "O you whom my soul loves," by the inspiration of your grace and by inspired experience, speak to my soul, for it is your lover, and tell me what state of mind it is, what sweetness is felt, what gladness is enjoyed when, to the faith that loves you insofar as faith can love, is given an inkling of that vision, insofar as an inkling of it can be given in this mortal life, and when that comes to pass in the lover which you once said of such a one, "He who loves me will be loved by my Father, and I will love him and manifest myself to him."[15] For when one day the lover, by loving thus, is somewhat more deserving of a loftier grace, he begins indeed to be loved. Hence by the sense of enlightened love, the Bride begins to experience more fully and dearly the sweet charms of the love of the Bridegroom who loves her. In her are accomplished the words of the Apostle: "The charity of God is poured forth in our hearts by the Holy Spirit who has been given to us."[16] For now she begins to know even as she has first been known[17] and, in the degree of her knowledge, to love as she has first been loved. For from the Bridegroom to the Bride, that first knowledge was a gift from the divine Wisdom, and that first love a gratuitous infusion of the Holy Spirit. But from the Bride to the Bridegroom, knowledge and love are all the same; for here love itself is understanding.[18]

---

15. Jn 14:21.　　　　16. Rom 5:5.　　　　17. Cf. 1 Cor 13:12.

18. "Love itself is understanding." William returns to this favorite concept again in no. 64: "To know him by loving him," and no. 76: "For love of God itself is knowledge of him; unless he is loved he is not known." We find this same theme in the *Mirror of Faith* (trans. Webb and Walker, pp. 60ff.) and in *On Contemplating God,* no. 6. In his treatise *On the Nature and Dignity of Love,* ch. 6 (trans. Webb and Walker, p. 32), William compares divine love with the sense of sight, and in the *Mirror of Faith* he says: "The mind is the soul's internal sense faculty. Nevertheless, the noblest sense faculty, the keenest, most powerful intellect, appears to be love, on condition that it is pure, for it is by it, as by a sense faculty, that the Creator is perceived by the creature; it is that which, like an intellect, gives intelligence of God . . . ."—*ibid.*

When by a superabundance of grace this happens in the Bride's heart for an hour or for a moment, then that which she seeks so anxiously in this life comes to pass, namely the noontide repose of Bridegroom with Bride—the repose of midday light in the understanding, of midday fervor in love—in which, when love returns whence it came, the Bridegroom while himself feeding, also gives himself to her as food. The word "feeds"[19] has these two senses.

58. Or, take this interpretation: If, she says, you account me unworthy of your kiss or of your word or of the breath of your mouth, show me at least one of your friends in whom I may find the fervor of your love, not in the faint dawn of morning or the dusk of evening, but in the steady glow of midday light. Show me a friend in whose heart you may lie and repose and through whose intermediary you may feed me while he teaches me what he has learned from you.[20]

59. Or here is a last interpretation: The Bride desires to cling to the Bridegroom, but she is too weak. She seeks joy of heart in the light of his countenance,[21] but she is plunged in inner darkness. Failing to dispose herself inwardly for the affection she desires, having no peace within her, she is eager to go forth from herself and perform some outward act of affection, whereby she may find the Bridegroom whom she loves in good conscience, and he may feed her and repose with her.[22]

Part or all of that which we have set forth is what she desired to know when she said: "Show me, O you, whom my soul loves,

19. The word in the Vulgate text which William uses here is *pascit*. Bernard also develops this idea of the bridegroom "feeding" both actively and passively; cf. Sermon 71, nos. 5 and 6 of the *Sermons on the Song of Songs*.

20. Is this what William sought for in Bernard and finally went to Signy to find? Certainly it is in the monastic tradition to seek a spiritual father who can teach from the abundance of his own personal experience.

21. Cf. Ps 88:16.

22. This turning towards charitable activity (of which William will speak again; see *infra*, no. 198) when the graces and consolations of contemplation are withdrawn is also counseled by St Bernard in his Fifty-first Sermon on the Song of Songs, no. 2.

where you feed, where you have your couch in the midday."
60. "Lest I begin to wander after the flocks of your companions."
She has not begun to wander, but she is afraid of wandering. Up to
the present she has loved no one save the Bridegroom. If she loved
anyone else, she would not be the Bride. For the moving force in
our soul is love, and consequently she who loves but one person is
unmoved and wanders not. Moreover she who presses forward on
one straight path toward the goal of her desires does not wander or
err, but eventually reaches her end. Should she leave the path,
however, the field of error opens before her, and it has no end.
Error consists in proclaiming the false to be true. The Bride is
indeed still disturbed in her thoughts, which are "as the tents of
Cedar, as the curtains of Solomon," easily shifted about. Moreover
she is assailed by her concupiscences, as she says: "The sons of my
mother have fought against me." But love's judgment, ever
standing its ground, is not moved; it merely seeks to be enlightened
and desires to be strengthened. I love, says the Bride, or rather I
desire to love. For the eye of my mind is troubled by the urge of
concupiscence and the images of various thoughts, so that I see
not him whom I love. My reason is drowsy, and I understand not
what I desire. Therefore I falter and grow fickle in my love, not by
renouncing it but by pursuing it along divergent roads. And thus
I become inconstant in love, not by willing or refusing, but by seeking a shorter and easier path to attain that which I will firmly and
solely. For my will is ever the same, but until my good will becomes
equivalent to a good soul, my desire is incessant. Nevertheless, it
seems to me that my love is not incessant since, as I have said, what
I desire is not always present to my affection. For the love of him
who desires is not the same as the love of him who has fruition. The
love of desire burns even in the darkness but gives no light; whereas
the love of him who has fruition is wholly in the light, because
fruition itself is the light of the lover. Why say more? The Bride
who eagerly strives to see God desires a pure heart, a pure conscience, pure senses, pure understanding—complete purity. Neither

fire nor sword nor any kind of danger can disturb the strength of love,[23] but fruition of its delights calls for peace of heart and serenity of soul.

61. "Lest I begin to wander," she says, "after the flocks of your companions." Men who err not are aware how many flocks error has called together in the world—the countless individuals and whole nations who choose death instead of life, embrace misery instead of beatitude, neglect God, love themselves, follow the beaten paths of this world, throng into hell and leave their footprints behind them. For the prince of spiritual iniquity, who works on the children of disbelief, draws them in his train. He it was who posed as a friend of the Bridegroom and said: "I will be like the Most High!"[24] He is the prince of this world,[25] who appears to share the world and time on equal terms, as it were, with the Bridegroom. But the fact is that he draws to his side far greater flocks among the erring. And even in the heart of her who now deserves to be a Bride, it sometimes happens that her spiritual gaze wavers in the study of the unique truth and is straightway overtaken by a large number of different thoughts. Left free and beginning to wander among them, her mind is dragged away from itself down many paths of error and withdrawn by mental images from the rectitude of its good intentions. For these various thoughts, calling together various flocks of their own, pose as friends of the Bridegroom when they divide with him the soul of the Bride and force her to serve their turn, their opportunity and themselves.[26]

23. Cf. Rom 8:35.   24. Is 14:14.   25. Cf. Jn 12:31; 14:30; 16:11.

26. William was well aware of the danger (here) and the suffering (see *infra,* nos. 122, 144) that distractions can cause the man seeking contemplative union with God; yet he kept a very realistic view of them (see *infra,* no. 178). And to the brethren of Mont Dieu he gave this sound advice: "For thoughts which fall in, as it were, from without and pass out again, and fleeting motions of will whereby now he wills and now he wills not, are commonly to be reckoned not among motions of the will, but as idle thoughts. For though they sometimes proceed even to delectation of the mind, yet that mind which is the master of itself soon shakes itself free of them."—*Letter to the Carthusians of Mont Dieu,* no. 61, trans. Shewring, p. 105.

G

STANZA 5

If you know not yourself,
O fairest among women,
Go forth and depart, following after
   the steps of the flocks;
And feed your goats
Beside the tents of the shepherds.[1]

NEXT comes this: "If you know not yourself, O fairest among women, go forth and depart, following after the steps of the flocks." As if to say: What you ask me to show you, this you know; but you know not yourself. For you suppose you know me not, because you know not yourself. And you know not yourself because you have gone forth from yourself.

63. But first we must take note of the loving blandishments on both sides. The Bride says: "O you whom my soul loves!" And the Bridegroom: "O fairest among women, O my love!" When anyone, in the heat of temptation, believes he hears this dialogue of love and praise spoken in the truth of his conscience, this is no sign that he is forsaken or unfaithful. Blessed is the conscience which, whatever occurs, whatever happens, says always with the same spirit: "The Lord Jesus!"[2] and cries with the same piety: "O you whom my soul loves!" Blessed is this conscience whose faith, bearing testimony to the truth whatever befalls, loses none of its fairness and none of its praise. "Fairest," he says, "among women,"

1. Song 1:7.   2. Cor 12:3.

strong among the delicate, for the word "woman" *(mulier)* comes from "delicacy" *(mollities)*;[3] a virgin among those that are with child, whom the Lord doomed to woe when he said: "Woe to those who are with child or have infants at the breast in those days!"[4] Fairest, he says, because you are beautiful, that is, finely formed, inasmuch as your soul loves me through your being informed by grace; even though you are somewhat black, inasmuch as you are destitute of illuminating grace.

64. "If you know not yourself, O fairest among women, go forth!" This reminder of her fairness may be viewed as a reproach for her neglect of it. And he says: "Go forth!" This is not advice from a friend, but more like a concession on the part of an angry man. "If you know not yourself, go forth!" would therefore mean: If you go forth from yourself, it is because you know not yourself. Know yourself, then, to be my image; thus you can know me, whose image you are, and you will find me within you. If you are with me in your soul, there I will repose with you; and then I will feed you. Seek God therefore in simplicity,[5] think of him in

3. William here, as was common practice at that period, follows the etymology of St Isidore of Seville. Cf. *Etymologia*, 11:2:18; PL 82: 417a.

4. Mt 24:19.

5. Cf. Wis 1:1. This is one of the favorite texts of William. He returns to it again and again, e.g. *infra*, nos. 67, 70, 89, 115. In his *Letter to the Carthusians of Mont Dieu* William defines what he means by simplicity: "For in very truth simplicity is the perfect turning of the will to God, asking one thing from the Lord and seeking this, not turning hither and thither to the multiplicity in the world. Or again, simplicity is true humility in conversation, seeking a righteous conscience rather than fame, when the simple man fears not to seem foolish in the world that he may be wise in God. Again, simplicity is the turning of the naked will to God, but not yet formed by reason to be love, which is a formed will, not yet enlightened to be charity, which is the bliss of love"—no. 13, trans. Shewring, p. 29. Simplicity has been considered "a characteristic of the Cistercian Order" both as regards externals, as is evident for example from their Institutes (cf. *Little Exordium,* chs. 15 and 17, trans. Larkin, pp. 262ff.), their architecture, etc., and as an interior attitude of soul; see e.g. St Bernard's Third Sermon for the Feast of the Epiphany, no. 8: "For all of us in the beginning of our conversion no virtue is more necessary than humble simplicity."

goodness, strive to have him ever in your memory, to know him by loving him and to love him by knowing him; and in the thought of his goodness you shall perceive the sense of his eternity, and the manner of life and the state which befit the good soul.

65. "If you know not yourself, go forth!"—But, Lord, whither shall I go? When I go forth, when I am cast out like Cain from your face, the first one that finds me shall kill me.[6]

"Go forth and depart!"—as if he said: Depart from me, from my likeness, into the place of unlikeness![7] Depart, to put it plainly, from yourself, into the byways of concupiscence or curiosity. "Depart," therefore, "and feed your goats," which are allotted a place on the left hand, namely your lascivious impulses; let them feed elsewhere, but not in you. "Depart, following after the steps of the flocks" of the throng who are on their way to perdition; go forth to the pastures of those who feed themselves and love themselves. Depart toward the tents of those whose dwelling places are to all generations, who, as the psalmist says, have called their lands by other names[8] but have not caused their names to be written in heaven.[9]

66. But not so, Bride of Christ, not so. Nay rather, know yourself; be ready for discernment in your own regard. If you wish the

---

6. Cf. Gen 4:14.

7. Originating with Plato and Plotinus the idea of a land or region of unlikeness was adopted by Christian writers such as Eusebius, St Athanasius and St Augustine, until it is found to be of almost universal use in the Middle Ages. It is common among the Cistercian Fathers: e.g. St Bernard, Sermon 42 of the *Occasional Sermons*, no. 2 (PL 183: 1176); *Tract on Grace and Free Will*, ch. 10, no. 32 (*S. Bernardi Opera*, III [Rome: Editiones Cistercienses, 1963], p. 188); St Aelred, *Jesus at the Age of Twelve*, no. 3 (trans. T. Berkeley, in *The Works of Aelred of Rievaulx*, vol. 1 [Cistercian Fathers Series 2]; *Sermons on Isaiah*, Sermon 8 (PL 195:391). Most of these Christian authors associate the land of unlikeness with that far-away country in Luke 15:13 and thus the emphasis is on the notion of sin; however, sometimes, especially in the case of St Bernard, it is merely a question of the soul being an alien on earth, an exile in a land that is not its true country.

8. Cf. Ps 48:12.   9. Cf. Lk 10:20.

King, the Lord your God, to desire your beauty, draw near to him and forget your people and your father's house;[10] forget the material objects to which your bodily senses are accustomed, the pleasures derived from the things you clung to with love and the images pressed deep in your memory by the desire for enjoyment. Going forth from yourself in this way, you have departed from yourself, following with affection after the steps of your many purposes. You keep them so impressed on your memory that even when the objects are absent, their images remain; when the actions cease, the affections they aroused are still keen; when the sound of words is hushed, their sense continues to re-echo. Purify yourself, train yourself in godliness,[11] and you shall find the kingdom of God within you.[12] O image of God, recognize your dignity;[13] let the effigy of your Creator shine forth in you. To yourself you seem of little worth, but in reality you are precious. Insofar as you forsook him whose image you are, you have taken on the colors of strange images. But when you begin to breathe in the atmosphere wherein you were created, if perchance you embrace discipline,[14] you will quickly shake off and renounce this false make-up which is only superficial and not even skin-deep. Be wholly present to yourself, therefore, and employ yourself wholly in knowing yourself and knowing whose image you are, and likewise in discerning and understanding what you are and what you can do in him whose image you are. Stand in your rank; be not overcome, be not dishonored. The strength of your position is the knowledge of grace, if you are not ungrateful that you were foreseen, predestined, preferred and foreknown. For God's foreknowledge in your regard is his goodness toward you; predestination is his goodness now at work; preference is the work itself; and knowledge is the seal of

10. Cf. Ps 44:11f.　　11. Cf. 1 Tim 4:7.　　12. Cf. Lk 17:21.

13. This call for the Christian to recognize his dignity is drawn from tradition. See e.g. Pope St Leo, Sermon 21 for the Feast of Christmas: *Agnosce, O Christiane, dignitatem tuam.*

14. Cf. Ps 2:12.

grace, of which the Apostle says: "But the sure foundation of God stands firm, bearing this seal: 'The Lord knows who are his'."[15] If you know, be sure that you were foreknown; if you choose, be sure that you were chosen; if you believe, you were created for faith; and if you love, you were formed for love. And since the Bridegroom made you to be a Bride, he reposes in you; and since he attracts you, you recline with him and he feeds you. There it is that experience of the light and warmth of midday instructs you, when light is seen in God's light,[16] when, from the greatness and purity of love, the Holy Spirit gives testimony to a man's conscience that he is a son of God.[17] "No one knows the Father except the Son, and him to whom the Son chooses to reveal him."[18]

67. The light of God's countenance is the only light that teaches this;[19] the sense of life, from the Spirit of life, discloses it; it is grace for grace;[20] it is the immense fruition of the highest Good in reward for immense desire. The soul will never know itself (what it is and what it is capable of) unless it finds itself in this light and by this sense of life; nor may it go forth from itself to be somewhere else when in this light and by this sense of life, it is given it to find happiness in itself. Blessed is the man, happy is he, who has this glory and the wealth of this grace in the house of his heart and the treasure chamber of his conscience. His heart is strengthened; he shall not be moved.[21] That is, he will not go forth after strange things by covetousness or by actions bred of curiosity. He is rich at home, possessing peace and godliness with contentment in a good conscience.[22] This is the wealth of the poor in spirit[23] who seek God in simplicity of heart.[24] They perform with constancy what is commanded, await with strong faith what is promised, anticipate in the certainty of hope what is awaited and therefore think of God

15. 2 Tim 2:19. 16. Cf. Ps 35:10. 17. Cf. Rom 8:16.
18. Mt 11:27. 19. Cf. Ps 88:16. 20. Cf. Jn 1:16.
21. These last two sentences have been inspired by several verses of Ps 111.
22. Cf. 1 Tim 6:6. 23. Cf. Mt 5:3. 24. Cf. Wis 1:1.

in goodness.[25] They set not their minds on high things but condescend to the lowly;[26] they neither refuse the Lord's yoke nor kick against the goad of his discipline.[27] All this is far from the spirit of the world and its peddling[28] wisdom, Assyrian conceit and ornamental eloquence.

68. The poor of spirit are your horsemen, O you who rule Israel not with the horses of pride and the chariots of vanity but in the name of the Lord,[29] in the speed of the swift Spirit and by the strength of your love. The Hebrews (that is, they who pass over), knowing that they had been saved by you from the destroyer (which is the meaning of the name "Pharaoh") and from the region of darkness (which is Egypt),[30] in the shedding of blood and the sacrament of the Paschal Lamb, celebrate in haste the Pasch, that is the Passover of the Lord,[31] by passing from vice to virtue, from the things of time to the things of eternity, from earth to heaven, from themselves to God, while the sins and vices that pursued them are drowned in the waters reddened by the blood of the Lamb.[32] In adversity, as in the terror of the night,[33] they have for light, like the pillar of fire, the fire and strength of the Holy Spirit; but in prosperity, as in daylight, they have the power of the Most High overshadowing them like the cloud.[34]

---

25. *Ibid.*   26. Cf. Ps 130; Rom 12:16.   27. Cf. Mt 11:29; Acts 9:5.

28. William uses here an unusual word: *nugigerula ejus sapientia.* It is found also in his *Letter to the Carthusians of Mont Dieu,* no. 52, trans. Shewring, p. 93.

29. Cf. Ps 79:2; 19:8.

30. Ex 2:22. This spiritual interpretation of Pharaoh and Egypt is common among the Cistercian Fathers; see e.g. St Aelred's Second Sermon for the Feast of St Benedict, trans. M. Basil Pennington, in *Cistercian Studies,* 4 (1969), pp. 62ff., especially p. 73.

31. Cf. Ex 12:11.   32. Cf. Ex 14:28.

33. Cf. Ps 90:5.   34. Cf. Ex 13:21f.; Lk 1:35.

STANZA 6

To my company of horsemen,
  in Pharaoh's chariots,
Have I likened you, O my love!

Your cheeks are beautiful as the turtledove's,
Your neck as jewels.

We will make you chains of gold,
Inlaid with silver.[1]

THEREFORE the Bridegroom continues in these terms:
"To my company of horsemen, in Pharaoh's chariots, have I
likened you, O my love!" We must not pass over the fact
that he calls her first beautiful among women and, after that, his love.
He includes everything in these two expressions to make us understand that the degree of beauty will determine the mode of friendship. By these words—"To my company of horsemen have I
likened you, O my love!"—the tender wisdom of the Bridegroom
adds to the favors already given the Bride yet another, by recalling
her to herself just as she was going forth from herself. And in this
particular, where she thought herself wisest, he rebukes her for the
greater folly, warning her that life is endangered and love injured
when she seeks only love's delights and shuns its labors. Indeed this is
what usually happens to beginners; spiritual carelessness envelops

1. Song 1:8ff.

their frail and unwary souls and prevents them from attaining the goal of perfection. At the slightest taste of the new sweets of contemplation and its sweeter experiences they immediately suppose that they have passed beyond all need of contending with the vices of flesh and spirit. They dream of nothing but the charms of the virtues, which are naturally delightful; and they take no trouble to possess the virtues truly and securely, disdaining the need to practice them. Trusting in the sweetness they have tasted (which comes rather from God who shows mercy than from him who wills or him who runs),[2] they pay no heed to serious dangers arising from their side and preying upon them from within. The Bridegroom, therefore, once the way of purity has been revealed and the door of freedom in contemplation opened, goes on to add these words: "To my company of horsemen, in Pharaoh's chariots, have I likened you, O my love!" Even though you are my love, and very truly my love, nevertheless be assured that you must still ride and press forward, and labor and fight; and this will not make you any less my love. But you must shun the vice of curiosity and the concupiscence of the world and of the flesh which invariably goes with it; and yet for yourself or your brethren, you must not refuse works of obligation or the obligations of charity.[3]

70. Next comes this text: "Your cheeks are beautiful as the turtledove's." The Bride's cheeks, and her face, which is ever unveiled for the Bridegroom, denote her pure conscience. The modesty shining on her face is her loving repentance and tender reverence for him who has just rebuked her. The faithful soul, indeed, while she is laboring in temptations, knows not what is taking place within her; often she makes progress without being aware of it, and she is favored when she thinks herself rejected. In

2. Cf. Rom 9:16.

3. St Bernard is equally if not more insistent on this obligation of the true contemplative to answer to the demands of charity. See esp. Sermons 51 and 57 on the Song of Songs.

her affliction she humbles herself, and in her humility she is purified.
Deep within her, the practice of humility fosters lowliness; at the
same time, amid many sufferings, there takes shape within her
(even though not through her own efforts) that holy simplicity of
which Scripture says: "Seek the Lord in simplicity of heart."[4]
And when she considers herself worthy of rebukes and affliction,
her devout conscience takes on, before him who rebukes her, a
pure and pleasing modesty of face, thus making amends for her
former impudence and presumption. This is why she now deserves
to hear these words: "Your cheeks are beautiful as the turtledove's."
Observe that at the moment when temptation reaches its height,
the remedy of divine comfort is suddenly at hand within her; and
according to the multitude of sorrows in her heart, the comforts
of the Lord are at hand, giving joy to her soul.[5] In the time of her
rebellion, her soul being attracted to the flesh and her flesh being
attracted to sin, gave her the face of a vulture; but in the hour of
the visitation of grace, her soul being attracted to God and her
flesh being attracted to the soul, gave her the face of a turtledove,
displaying humility, chastity and the grace of holy simplicity. For
just as conscience is its own truest interpreter of the attraction of
grace, so the outward face is ordinarily the witness before men of
a well-disposed conscience.[6] Furthermore a blush appearing on
the face is usually a sign of some good thought hidden in the heart.
For when, through the sense of sight, the soul is confronted with
something it considers itself unworthy to see, it takes refuge within,
as physicians say, screening itself behind its natural covering of
blood, which at that very moment reddens the cheeks with con-
fusion, attesting the soul's inner modesty, that is, its hatred of the
shameful object presented, or its humility and shyness before the

4. Wis 1:1.

5. Cf. Ps 93:1.

6. St Bernard makes the same point in one of his sermons, *Occasional
Sermons*, 40:6; *The Works of Bernard of Clairvaux*, vol. 12 (Cistercian Fathers
Series 34).

homage offered it. And most fittingly is the Bride compared to a turtledove, which after losing its mate does not seek another but takes comfort in solitary lamentation.[7]

71. The Bride has been proved and found worthy; and now in the light of illuminating grace she sees herself exalted the more by the praises the Bridegroom willingly confers on her; that is, she is loaded with gifts answering to his praise. This is why he goes on to say: "Your neck is as jewels." The Bride's neck denotes her pure intention; the whole body of her work is joined to her head which is Christ.[8] Hence the same Christ our Head declares: "If your eye," that is, the intention of your work, "be sound, your whole body will be full of light."[9] As jewels are the adornment of the neck, so the precious stones of holy virtues are the adornment of our good intention. The Bride's neck is as jewels; it is "as" jewels, and this means that whereas the purpose of jewels is to adorn the neck, in this case it is the Bride's neck that adorns all her virtues. For unless virtues hang from the necklace of a right intention, it is impossible to prove their grace or beauty, or even their right to the name of virtues. Or it may be said that the adornment of the Bride's neck is love of the Bridegroom, without which every intention is impure and perverted. But when the Bride's intention is transformed into love, her neck becomes as its jewels.

72. Then, as if decking her with his own adornments, the Bridegroom says: "We will make you chains of gold, inlaid with silver." By "gold" we are to understand wisdom, because, as the Apostle says, "Christ has become for us wisdom,"[10]—either at the time when "being made like unto men and appearing in the form of man,"[11] his weakness appeared stronger than men and his foolishness wiser than men;[12] or at the time when we began to adhere to him, that in him we might be wise. He himself therefore adorns the Bride's

7. St Bernard develops more at length this comparison with the turtledove in his Fifty-ninth Sermon on the Song of Songs.
8. Cf. 1 Cor 11:3. 9. Mt 6:22. 10. 1 Cor 1:30.
11. Phil 2:7. 12. Cf. 1 Cor 1:25.

neck with ornaments of gold, when he adds to her pure intention the grace of wisdom, that her endeavors may be not only ardent but wise. These ornaments are inlaid with silver, when the Bride receives the grace of splendid and sonorous eloquence to proclaim the Bridegroom's glory and thereupon orders her words with judgment.[13] Inasmuch as the chains are silver, they signify, as we have said, the luster of eloquence; by their length they represent perseverance in good works; and by their roundness, perfection. But why are they inlaid? So that by the inlay, which is wrought in a wormlike pattern, eloquence may be reminded to beware of vanity. Every kind of tree and every kind of fruit has a worm of its own which is the natural enemy of its sound condition. In the same way every virtue and due balance of soul finds an enemy of its own among the vices. Hence it is written:"The worm of riches is pride."[14] As pride is the worm of riches, so vanity is the worm of eloquence; unless we beware of vanity, whatever beauty, strength or usefulness our eloquence may appear to have will certainly be brought to naught. Length, roundness and the other attributes of the necklace all inhere in the substance of the gold. And indeed there is no perseverance in good, no perfection, no beauty, no usefulness, unless they are established upon wisdom, that is, upon the love of God and spiritual sense.

73. But he says: "We will make." Should "we" be understood here as singular or plural? Assuredly it refers to him who said, speaking of his lover, "We will come to him and make our abode with him."[15] So it is the Lord Jesus Christ, and God the Father and the Holy Spirit.

Or put it thus: I, he says, will make this necklace by the ministry of angels serving me in this task. For the angels, in their devotion, rejoice in the welfare of men and love to serve in the work of their salvation; they are always ready to aid them in the holy labors of

13. Cf. Ps 111:5.   14. The source of this citation is unknown.
15. Jn 14:23.

religion, although they do not always appear visibly. If then they are sometimes unexpectedly seen by certain men, they are said to appear; this word properly applies to an object present but concealed, which suddenly shows itself visibly. The spiritual power of the angel has a certain natural faculty of suggesting or imparting, to another angel or to the minds of men, all sorts of thoughts. This is what the prophet Zechariah meant when he said: "The angel that spoke in me went forth," and: "One angel said to the other angel: Run and speak to this young man."[16] These secret beckonings, by which the good angels, according to God's will, convey suggestions for good and the bad angels, by his permission, for evil, seem to be called by the Apostle "the angels' tongues," for he says: "If I should speak with the tongues of angels, but do not have charity . . . I am nothing."[17] God's angels are always present, by their encouragement and cooperation, to the holy labors of proficients. They share the Bride's joy in her spiritual ornaments more and more as they recognize therein the works of God's fingers and the art of the Holy Spirit. And we must understand that the angels are not alone in this; the holy doctors also, in God's Church, have cooperated with the Bridegroom for the bridal adornments.

16. Zech 2:3f.   17. 1 Cor 13:1.

STANZA 7

While the King was at his repose,
My spikenard sent forth its fragrance.

A nosegay of myrrh is my Beloved to me;
He shall abide between my breasts.

A cluster of cypress, my Love is to me;
In the vineyards of Engaddi.[1]

NEXT: "While the King was at his repose, my spikenard sent forth its fragrance." Men who are skilled in archery tell us the hand of the archer possesses a kind of sense by which, even after the arrow is out of sight, he is often aware that his shot will reach the mark. In the same way all agree that a faithful soul who prays faithfully sometimes possesses a kind of sense of tender piety by which it is aware of the moment when its prayer comes before God; and from the answer of illuminating grace and the sense of its good conscience, it no longer doubts that it is heard. The Bride has now been instructed by the Master's chastisement and correction and glorified by the gift of wisdom; clothing herself therefore in affection, she begins to know herself more perfectly and to understand and discern what is taking place within her. And now at the Bridegroom's indication, that is by illuminating grace, she begins to find within herself what she had been seeking as if it were

1. Song 1:11ff.

elsewhere, when she said: "Show me, O you whom my soul loves, where you feed, where you have your couch in the midday?" In other words, she begins to contemplate the kingdom of God within her[2]—a place for the Lord, a tabernacle for the God of Jacob.[3] This is not the kind of contemplation which she had first attempted with the presumption of novice fervor and which, having received it as a free favor, she had expended with more ardor than wisdom. Rather it is that contemplation which begins to open out of itself in her, now that she has been proved by temptations, instructed by chastisement and correction, and illumined by the merit of a purer conscience.[4]

75. This leads the Bride to continue as follows: "While the King was at his repose, my spikenard sent forth its fragrance." When lovers repose together, they may do so in two different ways: either to participate in the pleasures of the flesh, or to receive food. The Bride was seeking both these things, but in the spiritual order, when a short while previously she asked: "Show me where you feed, where you have your couch in the midday."

76. Now the place where Bridegroom and Bride lie down or repose is her memory, her understanding and her love. For it is in these faculties that Bridegroom and Bride repose together; he, that is, infuses grace, and she cherishes tender memories, comprehends with humility and loves with ardor. This is the place sought with anxious devotion by him who said: "If I shall give sleep to my eyes or slumber to my eyelids until I find a place for the Lord, a tabernacle for the God of Jacob."[5] His heart, insofar as it burned

---

2. Cf. Lk 17:21.   3. Cf. Ps 131:5.

4. William seems to be describing here the passage of the soul into the second state which he calls that of the progressive, or the rational state; see *supra*, no. 13; also the *Letter to the Carthusians of Mont Dieu*, no. 12, trans. Shewring, p. 26. It is common doctrine that a soul must pass through a period of purgation and active labor toward virtue before it can enter upon the way of illumination and contemplation; see e.g. St Bernard's Forty-sixth Sermon on the Song of Songs, no. 6.

5. Ps 131:4f.

with this holy desire, was assuredly a place of God already; but he
desired to stay there to enjoy him, to have continuous fruition.
Already his memory was filled and utterly possessed by a crucifying
will or desire, in other words a passionate will. But because understanding lacked its light, love had never been able to find its joy
in fruition. This is the joy of which the psalmist speaks farther on:
"We will go into his tabernacle: we will adore in the place where
his feet stood."[6] A person who prays to God and does not feel him
present (as he should be felt), prays with anxiety; but he who
possesses his presence, enjoys his presence and adores him with
rejoicing.

Therefore when the Bride remembered the Bridegroom, or
thought of him, seeking understanding she supposed him to be
absent as long as her understanding turned not into love. But
goodwill is already the beginning of love. And a passionate will,
directed as if to an absent person, is desire; drawn to someone present, it is love; then what the lover loves is present to his understanding. For love of God itself is knowledge of him; unless he is
loved, he is not known, and unless he is known, he is not loved.
He is known only insofar as he is loved, and he is loved only insofar
as he is known.

The Bridegroom therefore reposes with the Bride when by
gratuitous grace he first sanctifies in her her free will's adhesion to
him. But it does not seem to the Bride that she reposes with him
while her understanding finds not its joy in love, nor her love in
affectionate fruition; while she sings in spirit, but not with her
understanding; while her spirit sings or prays, but her understanding, as she sings or prays, is without fruit.[7] Hidden grace is
already working powerfully within her, but to her it seems not to
be so, until she comes to perfect love of him who brings it to pass
that she is reposing with him in his repose. This is why she says:
"While the King was at his repose, my spikenard sent forth its
fragrance."

6. Ps 131:7.   7. Cf. 1 Cor 14:14f.

She says, "in his repose," not "in our repose." In other words, in this repose she is made a Bride by the Bridegroom, but is not yet drawn to him as she desires—as she will be later on when she says of the bed, "Our little bed is flowery."

77. "My spikenard sent forth its fragrance." Spikenard is a low-growing herb, with abundant foliage and ears; it is the symbol of humility, fruitful in virtues. It is hot, signifying the heat of holy desire. It is good for the making of perfumes, because in God's sight there is no loving devotion without the virtue of humility. It has an excellent odor—signifying, in humility, the confession of sins. We see this in the alabaster jar of genuine nard or precious ointment, which the humble devotion of a woman poured upon Jesus's body, anointing it in advance for burial. Hence concerning the fragrance of the humble nard, that is, of devout confession, the Gospel adds: "And the house was filled with the odor of the ointment."[8]

78. The Bride says: I was seeking him outside myself, as if he were absent, whereas I already possessed him reposing and feeding within me. The devotion of goodwill gave proof of his repose within my heart; and the outpouring of confession, pleasing to God, bore witness that he was feeding me interiorly by operating grace. But I knew not where he was feeding or where he made his couch. The firm consent of my will and the judgment of my reason brought all this to pass within me; but I possessed not the sense of spiritual affection by which the sweetness of his presence is perceived.

79. Then the Bride describes the favor of spiritual repose more exactly. First she adds that in thanksgiving she gathers up in her memory the remembrance of all the delights she has experienced, for she says: "A nosegay of myrrh is my Beloved to me; he shall abide between my breasts." Then she opens the eyes of the spiritual understanding to the light of grace and says: "A cluster of cypress

8. Jn 12:3.

H

my Love is to me." And, associating her sweetness with the sense
of love, she says: "In the vineyards of Engaddi." For a memory that
is not ungrateful for God's benefits swiftly merits the joy of spiritual
understanding; and this spiritual understanding at once becomes
open to sweet experiences of love, less by knowledge than by
delight.

80. For the spiritual understanding, when it begins to be enlightened by the more abundant grace of the Holy Spirit, operates
in the human soul in a manner as different from that of the human
understanding as the nature of uncircumscribed light differs in
sublimity from the nature of the soul itself. For by the natural
understanding the soul grasps the object which it penetrates; but by
the spiritual understanding, instead of grasping, it is itself grasped.
For the object which it grasps by the natural understanding, it
discerns by the use of reason; but what it is unable to see into, it
cannot discern. For as the Holy Spirit breathes where he will, he
breathes when he will, however he will and as much as he will.
Man indeed hears his voice, in other words he feels the grace of him
who operates, but he knows not whence he comes or whither he
goes,[9] for neither the beginning nor the end nor the manner of this
operation depends on his power or good pleasure. A man knows
not whence the Spirit comes or whither he goes, when there comes
to him the sensible experience of a certain joy and of illuminating and
beatifying grace, which only enlightened love is permitted to feel;
a certain sweetness, that love both merits and brings about—a
sweetness unknown to the ordinary understanding but felt by
affection; the most firm substance of things to be hoped for, the
evidence of things that are not seen;[10] a testimony to Christian
faith, the faithful testimony of the Lord, giving wisdom to little
ones.[11] For the sweetness of God so manifests itself to the taste of
one who tastes it, that everything relating to the soul, the flesh, the
world or any created being becomes insipid to him; so that he

9. Cf. Jn 3:8.   10. Cf. Heb 11:1.   11. Cf. Ps 18:8.

would gladly die on the spot, while he is permitted to linger there. For as he feels that which he knows not, he prays without knowing what he asks, because it is the Spirit who pleads for him, according to God, not according to man,[12] and who makes him feel, plead for and desire the very thing which he knew not by feeling and felt without knowing. For only he who searches the heart knows what the Spirit desires,[13] that is to say, what he makes the desirous soul desire. This is what comes to pass with or in the soul that has merited to be a Bride, when from among the events of which the Lord said: "That which concerns me is at its end"[14] (that is, the divine dispensation concerning our Lord's humanity), and from the manifold benefits which have issued from them for us, she puts together a creed. This is like a nosegay of myrrh which she gives a place between her breasts, in her heart, in the safe abode of her memory and in the tenderness of her loving conscience. Here hostile temptation finds no easy access, and this very tenderness of love cannot abide the slightest injury to faith.

81. Myrrh is used to embalm the bodies of the dead.[15] Its taste is bitter like the bitterness of the passion which the Lord suffered for our sakes; and its fragrance is good like the sweetness of the love with which he loved us. And see the pleasing delights of spiritual love: after the jewels and chains, after the gift of wisdom, after the favor of eloquence, there is added as it were a little nosegay, to be fastened on the Bride's breast, that it may touch her devout memory with the sweetness of lasting perfume and ever breathe forth the charity of the Lord's sufferings and death. For it is a natural property

---

12. Cf. Rom 8:26f.   13. *Ibid.*; cf. also Ps7:10.   14. Cf. Lk 22:57.

15. In this and the following paragraph we find a great affinity to St Bernard's Forty-third Sermon on the Song of Songs. Devotion to the sacred humanity through meditation on his mysteries especially the passion is one of the characteristics of the Cistercian school of spirituality. Aelred of Rievaulx insists upon it strongly when writing a rule of life for his sister and composes a very beautiful meditation; see *The Life of the Recluse*, trans. Sr M. Paul, in *The Works of Aelred of Rievaulx*, vol. 1 (Cistercian Fathers Series 2), nos. 29f.

of myrrh that its taste is supposed to strengthen the power of the memory.

82. A "nosegay," not a bundle, because no human strength might bear the whole burden of the Lord's passion. It is indeed a nosegay of delights. One who wears it is not weighed down but rather sustained by devoutly remembering and sweetly considering the goodness of him who suffered, the cause of his sufferings and the sweetness of his love—the mystery of redemption, the example of humility, the challenge of charity and the power of resurrection. But if, as the Apostle says, "we neglect so great a salvation,"[16] and if on doomsday the Crucified calls us to account for his cross, his passion and his blood trodden underfoot, "O Lord, Lord, who shall stand it?"[17] "Dreadful" is that "expectation of judgment . . . which will consume the adversaries!"[18] Moreover if anyone, trusting in the power of his natural reason to penetrate the most lofty mystery of the two natures in Christ, seeks or ambitions things too high for him, he takes upon himself a heavy burden by which he must needs be overwhelmed. For, as the Apostle says, great is that mystery of godliness in Christ; although manifested in the flesh, it was justified only in the Spirit.[19] In other words, for the justice which is the fruit of faith, no reason adequate to its sublimity can be given to man or through man, except him to whom the Holy Spirit deigns to reveal it.[20]

83. Bearing her nosegay, the Bride toils not, because she loves; for a lover toils not. Besides, the remembrance of the Bridegroom, as the text says, is placed and abides between the Bride's breasts, so that the children of the Bridegroom may suck therefrom the milk of sacred nourishment. For these two breasts of the Bride are wisdom and knowledge,[21] of which the Apostle says: "To one

16. Heb 2:3.   17. Ps. 129:3   18. Heb 10:27.
19. Cf. 1 Tim 3:16.   20. Cf. Mt 11:27.

21. The breasts of the spouse for Bernard are encouragement and consolation, but like William they are meant to support the true life of the children. Cf. St Bernard's *Sermons on the Song of Songs*, Sermon 10.

through the Spirit is given the utterance of wisdom, and to another the utterance of knowledge."[22] For from these the children of the Bridegroom draw the support of true life, that is, the love of God. Created as we were to the image and likeness of the Creator,[23] we fell through our sin from God into ourselves, and fell from ourselves beneath ourselves into such an abyss of unlikeness that no hope was left. But there came the Son of God, eternal Wisdom; he bowed his heavens and came down.[24] He made of himself a being who should be among us[25] and like to us, so that we might grasp him; and he made that we be like to himself, so that we might be exalted by him. Thus the constant remembrance of this mystery would be our perpetual remedy. The nosegay of myrrh is what we grasp, but it is the cluster of cypress by which we are exalted. Of this the Bride adds: "A cluster of cypress my Love is to me: in the vineyard of Engaddi."

84. Wine gladdens those whom the bitterness of myrrh saddens. In the myrrh is to be understood the bitterness of the passion; in the wine of the grape, the joy of the resurrection. In the nosegay of myrrh, the faithful memory perceives whatever there was in Christ of human passibility and mortality; in the wine of the grape, hope and understanding discover the joy imparted by the power of the resurrection; and in the vineyards and balsam of Engaddi, love sees the anointing of the Spirit from the Holy One and joy in the Holy Spirit.

85. There is a great difference, however, between Cyprus, an island in the sea, and Engaddi, a place in Judea, both in their physical contrasts and in the unlikeness of the species of plants they produce. For Cyprus is renowned for its fertile vineyards; Engaddi, for its fine balsam. But they are coupled together in the same mystery of godliness: the grapes of Cyprus and the joy-giving wine temper the bitterness of the myrrh of sorrow of the passion, through the power

22. I Cor 12:8.   23. Cf. Gen 1:26f.
24. Cf. Ps 17:10.   25. Cf. Jn 1:14.

and joy of the resurrection; and the balsam of Engaddi is joined in it, to the end of consummating and perfecting all things, through the infusion of the Holy Spirit.

86. The nosegay of myrrh and the cluster of cypress abide between the Bride's breasts when her memory, lovingly drawn to the Bridegroom, is sometimes borne down by the myrrh and sometimes sustained by the cluster of grapes. Both these effects, however, require the balsam of Engaddi, that is, the visit of the grace of the Holy Spirit to attract the memory, enlighten the understanding and enkindle love. The cluster, with its large number of grapes, is an image of the joys to be found in the remembrance of the Bridegroom, and the name Cyprus indicates their rare quality. The balsam of Engaddi, however, indicates something much greater and of more worth than any wine (that is to say, much greater and of more worth than any of the joys of this life), namely the oil of gladness and the unction of the Holy Spirit wherewith God the Father anointed the Bridegroom, who is also God, above his fellows.[26] For whatever comes from faith and hope, from the memory and the intellect, seems to possess a certain feeling of love and joy; but joy in the Holy Spirit, in the fullness of love, conduces to a certain effective beatitude that surpasses all joy; it attains to what eye has not seen nor ear heard, to what has not entered into the heart of man,[27] in that city of God whereof we read in the psalm: "The dwelling in you is as it were of all rejoicing."[28] The expression, "As it were of all rejoicing," is used, for there is question not merely of rejoicing but of more than rejoicing. That joy has no name, unless we call it quasi-joy or super-joy. What seems to confirm this interpretation is that the vineyards of Cyprus and the vineyards of Engaddi do appear to have some resemblance; but, as we have said, they differ greatly in the excellence of their species of plants. The stalks of balsam do appear to resemble vine stalks, insofar as they are sometimes seen to stand two cubits high; but

26. Cf. Ps 44:8.   27. Cf. 1 Cor 2:9.   28. Ps 86:7.

they stand without the help of support, as vines cannot do. The seed of balsam also appears to resemble the vine in smell and taste. But in the perpetual glory of their foliage the stalks of balsam surpass the vines and display or symbolize the joy of eternal life, which, in order to subsist, has no need of help, because it is sustained solely by what it derives from itself.

87. Moreover the name Engaddi may be taken to mean "the fountain of the goat" or "the fountain of grace"; the goat, crossing it from left to right, becomes a lamb.[29] For the lambs are placed on the right hand, but the goats on the left.[30] When the branch of the balsam tree is pierced, the balsam is brought forth; this is a symbol of the sacrament flowing forth from the piercing of the Lord's side.[31] It is also a symbol of the remission of sins which proceeds from "compunction" of heart, and an echo of Solomon's words: "He that pricks the eye brings out tears; and he that pricks the heart lays bare its feelings."[32]

---

29. While St Bernard interprets the fountain of the goat as being the baptism of the nations, yet he applies to it the same effect; the goat crossing it becomes a lamb. Cf. St Bernard's *Sermons on the Song of Songs*, Sermon 44, nos. 1 and 7.

30. Cf. Mt 25:33.   31. Cf. Jn 19:34.   32. Sir 22:24.

STANZA 8

Behold you are fair, O my Love,
   behold you are fair:
Your eyes are as those of doves!

Behold you are fair, my Beloved, and comely!

Our little bed is flowery.
The beams of our houses are of cedar,
The rafters of cypress trees.[1]

T HE TEXT continues: "Behold you are fair, O my love, behold you are fair!" "Behold"—that is to say, in this attraction of devotion, in this manner of praise, in this beauty of perfection—in the image of God. For man was created to the image of God for this purpose, that, devoutly mindful of God in order to understand him, humbly understanding him in order to love him and loving him with ardor and wisdom until he attains to possession and fruition of him, he might be a rational animal.[2] For this is to fear God and keep his commandments, which is the whole duty of man.[3] And this is the image and likeness of God in man; of course, in a matter so unlike the divine Being, this image and likeness can exist only in a certain manner and to a certain extent.

---

1. Song 1:14ff.
2. William is referring to a particular state of the soul or a particular state of prayer. Cf. *supra*, no. 13, 16 ff.; also his *Letter to the Carthusians of Mont Dieu*, no. 12.   3 Cf. Eccles 12:13.

89. This likeness is most assuredly reason, by which man differs from the brute. For not to remember God is the nature of the brute; to remember him without seeking to understand him, is something more than the nature of the brute, but less than that of man. To remember him and seek to understand him is the nature of man; to understand him and therefore to love him, and by loving him to enjoy him and delight in him is proper to human reason in its perfection. Yes, the devout memory with swift enlightenment leads to a certain understanding or reasoned thought concerning God; pure understanding or reasoned thought at once warms into love; and love, by the attraction of the good, is straightway clothed in an image of the highest Good, in the manner and to the extent corresponding to its own nature and worth. This image is present to the good memory by assent; to the pure intellect by thought; to affectionate love by enjoyment and delight. It is present to love—that is, to the loving Bride—by the attitude of her soul; but to others, by the eager longing of their good will. As for the Bride, she remembers the Bridegroom when she seeks him in simplicity of heart; she understands him when she thinks of him in goodness;[4] and she loves him when she holds him in affection, when she enjoys him and delights in him, and when she is as he himself is.

90. When the Bridegroom finds the Bride in this state or attitude of soul, he says: "Behold you are fair, O my love, behold you are fair!" For whatever in the Bride's beauty had been discolored, has now been recolored by the Sun of justice; and whatever had lost its warmth in his absence, is now restored to warmth by his presence. For the Bride's substance, of which the Apostle says: "Faith is the substance of things to be hoped for",[5] has its own exceedingly beautiful colors, namely, the holy virtues, which, as we have already remarked,[6] lose their colors in her or regain them according as they are devoid of illuminating grace or enlightened by it.

---

4. Cf. Wis 1:1.   5. Heb 11:1.   6. Cf. *supra*, no. 47.

91. The Bridegroom therefore, admiring the Bride's face with its regained colors, raises his voice in praise of her and says: "Behold you are fair, O my love, behold you are fair!" The repetition signifies the actual fact of her beauty and its continual enhancement. Or again, it signifies this: you are fair in deeds, fair in affection. You are fair because you are beautiful, that is, finely formed; you are fair of color. Then behold, he says, while you purify your memory for me, humble your understanding before me and give me your love, you are fair, O my love, behold you are fair; and you are my love inasmuch as you are fair.

92. Since the perfection of contemplation consists in all these things, he adds concerning the Bride: "Your eyes are as those of doves!" Contemplation has two eyes, reason and love, as the prophet says: "the riches of salvation are wisdom and knowledge."[7] One of these eyes searches the things of men, according to knowledge; but the other searches divine things, according to wisdom. And when they are illumined by grace, they are of great mutual assistance, because love gives life to reason and reason gives light to love; thus their gaze becomes simple as the dove's in contemplation and prudent in circumspection. Often when these two eyes faithfully cooperate, they become one; in the contemplation of God, where love is chiefly operative, reason passes into love and is transformed into a certain spiritual and divine understanding which transcends and absorbs all reason. It is concerning this understanding that the Bride says to the Bridegroom further on: "You have wounded my heart with one of your eyes, and with one hair of your neck!"[8]

93. Now that the Bride has received praise from the Bridegroom for her beauty, she offers him the same commendation and says: "Behold you are fair, my Beloved, and comely!" It is indeed an exchange of compliments when the Bride is called "fair," and again "fair" and "love," and the Bridegroom also is called "fair," and

7. Cf. Is 33:6.   8. Song 4:9.

"comely" and "Beloved." Henceforth having been taught by temptations, purified by penitence and divinely enlightened, the Bride begins to know herself and to find within herself him whom she was seeking. And now Bridegroom and Bride, in loving companionship and familiar conversation, ingratiating themselves with one another, giving pleasure to one another and praising one another, gain a foretaste of the joy of their mutual union. So while love's affairs are being transacted and making gradual progress in all respects, according to the measure of perfection granted by God, Bridegroom and Bride converse with one another. The Bride's part is devout affection; and the Bridegroom's, the effective work of operating grace. In other words, the Bridegroom's discourse is the work of "attracting" grace, and the Bride's reply is the very joy of a well "attracted" conscience. Or we may put it thus: for the Bride, to speak to the Bridegroom is to show herself in his eyes such as she is; and for the Bridegroom to speak to the Bride is to set in order and dispose the Bride herself, or what pertains to her, in her own understanding. Whatever the Bridegroom says in praise of the Bride is also testimony of her holy conscience; and what the Bride says in praise of the Bridegroom is the attraction of devotion and the love of contemplation. For no one possessed of a glimmer of reason harbors in his soul such perversion, or such aversion to God, that God does not sometimes speak within him. How much more will he not speak within the Bride, in view of the fact that as a woman with her husband is one flesh, the Bride with God is one spirit?[9]

94. When therefore the Bride has been called "fair," and again "fair" and "love," she is not ungrateful in devotion but reciprocates the Bridegroom's praises and calls him "fair" and "comely" and "Beloved." In other words she understands and is convinced that anything praiseworthy she has, she holds from him, who is the Good of all that is good and the Beauty of all that is beautiful. From

9. Cf. Gen 2:24; Mt 19:5.

him, praise is nothing else than the conferring of those qualities that merit praise. And what constitutes the reciprocal favor with which Bridegroom and Bride regard each other is their mutual resemblance in beauty and their mutual fruition which draws them together. For it is not only that we have fruition of God; God himself also enjoys our goodness, insofar as he delights in it and deigns to find it pleasing.[10] The degree of fruition becomes the degree of progress and likeness; because there can be no likeness apart from the fruition which accompanies it, and there can be no fruition apart from the likeness which brings it about. For whenever a soul receives, by God's gift, a certain grace for its own profit, it receives also, with that gift, understanding of the Giver; that man may not be ungrateful to God, but his turning may be toward the Giver. When humble love turns toward God more ardently, it is conformed to him toward whom it turns; because as it turns it is given by him an aptitude for such conformity. And since man is made in the likeness of his Maker, he becomes attracted to God; that is, he becomes one spirit with God, beautiful in his Beauty, good in his Goodness; and this takes place in proportion to the strength of his faith, the light of his understanding and the measure of his love. He is then in God, by grace, what God is by nature. For when, sometimes, grace superabounds to the point of a positive and evident experience of something of God, suddenly, in a new sort of way, something comes within the grasp of the sense of enlightened love which exceeds the reach of any bodily sense, the consideration of reason, and all understanding except the understanding of enlightened love. In this state, for this man of God, there is no difference between thus grasping something of God and (by the attraction of the happy experience) becoming like to him in accord with the nature both of the impression experienced and the love that experiences it.

On the level of the bodily senses, the act of sensation consists in perceiving in the mind, through a certain mental image, a certain

10. Cf. Gen 1:31.

likeness to the thing perceived in accordance with the nature both of the sense which perceives, and of the thing in question. If what is perceived pertains, for instance, to the sense of sight, it cannot be seen at all by him who sees, unless the visible element of it is first formed in the mind of him who sees, by the likeness of a certain image, through which he who perceives is transformed into the thing perceived. In this way, and to a much greater degree, the vision of God is brought about in the sense of love by which God is seen. Likewise even for bodily sensation, unless love also cooperates with the sense, the sense itself has hardly any effect; for he to whom the sense belongs is continually drawing back, unless by some urge of love he adheres to the thing perceived. But in the vision of God, where love alone is operative without the cooperation of any other sense, in a manner incomparably nobler and more refined than any imagination due to the senses, purity of love and the divine attraction play this same role; they arouse more sweetly him who perceives, they attract him more strongly and master him more gently; they transform the faithful lover wholly, mind and activity, into God, not only strengthening him, but conforming him and vivifying him that he may have fruition. Therefore the Bride immediately goes on to speak of fruition and says: "Our little bed is flowery."

95. The little flowery bed is a conscience full of charm, and the joy of the Holy Spirit in it; it is the constant fruition of truth in its very fountainhead. This is the bed of which the same Bridegroom says: "Upon whom shall my Spirit rest unless upon him who is humble and calm and who trembles at my words?"[11] It is pleasant to pause before the beauty of the flowery bed and consider its joyful pleasures—the springtime beauty of chastity and charity, the wafted fragrance of spiritual feelings and thoughts, the breath of the perfume of divinity and the strength of eternity. Upon this bed takes place that wonderful union and mutual fruition—of

11. Cf. Is 66:2.

sweetness, and of joy incomprehensible and inconceivable even to those in whom it takes place—between man and God, the created spirit and the Uncreated. They are named Bride and Bridegroom, while words are sought that may somehow express in human language the charm and sweetness of this union, which is nothing else than the unity of the Father and the Son of God, their Kiss, their Embrace, their Love, their Goodness and whatever in that supremely simple Unity is common to both. All this is the Holy Spirit—God, Charity, at once Giver and Gift. Upon this bed are exchanged that kiss and that embrace by which the Bride begins to know as she herself is known. And as happens in the kisses of lovers, who by a certain sweet, mutual exchange, impart their spirit each to the other, so the created spirit pours itself out wholly into the Spirit who creates it for this very effusion; and the Creator Spirit infuses himself into it as he wills, and man becomes one spirit with God.[12]

96. In the sorrows of the present life, this bed is the sole refuge for the children of the Bridegroom from persecutions and anguish; their only rest amid labors and their consolation amid sufferings; it is the mirror of life, the strength of faith, the pledge of hope and the sweet sustenance of love and charity in their advance toward God. That is why the vessel of election,[13] after telling us that he conducted himself as God's minister, "in much patience; in tribulations, in necessities and in distresses; in stripes, in prisons, in seditions; in labors, in sleepless nights, in fastings; in chastity, in knowledge, in long-suffering,"[14] proceeds—as though after the exhaustion caused by such great labors, he were seeking refuge in the little flowery bed and its quiet—to add these words: "in sweetness, in the Holy Spirit."[15]

97. Blessed is the conscience which, constantly seeking the face of the Lord, after the anguish of bodily labors, after the tribulations

---

12. Cf. 1 Cor 6:17   13. Cf. Acts 9:15.
14. 2 Cor 6:4ff.   15. 2 Cor 6:6.

of spiritual exercises, ever has ready deep within itself a domicile
of quiet and a little flowery bed. What is this but the inner joy of
its own testimony, of which the Doctor of the Gentiles also says:
"Our boast is this, the testimony of our conscience"?[16] No less
blessed is the conscience which leaves the joy of this interior
sweetness to perform some needful work at the command of
charity,[17] yet, no matter where it has been, always has the way prepared for its return home. But this is not always possible for one
who, whenever he must go forth, does so without reserve. For if
sometimes the tender nursling must quit his flowery bed to attend
to alien matters, nevertheless he must never become wholly alienated from it. He must always leave behind something of himself
which will faithfully keep his place for him; to which the part of
him forced to go forth must always cling by a strong bond of love,
that it may not stray too far away. Let the charity of truth always
remain there, even when some obligation of charity compels him
to go forth to attend to alien matters; and let not the force of outward obligations ever succeed in withdrawing the Bride's whole
soul from the enthrallment of inward sweetness.[18]

98. But when all iniquity passes away with the fashion of this
world,[19] all the aforesaid obligations will also pass away. Then the
union of Bridegroom and Bride will become full and abiding, in
the plenitude of likeness. Not only shall the Bridegroom be seen

16. 2 Cor 1:12.

17. This self-sacrificing responsiveness to the commands of charity, which
is an attitude of the true contemplative, William will speak of again (cf. *infra*)
nos. 136, 139). His friend St Bernard emphasized this quality also in his
Sermons on the Song of Songs; cf. Sermon 50, no. 5; 58, no. 2.

18. William takes care to note that the contemplative is not to go wholly
out of himself in this charitable service, but remain always a contemplative,
united in the depths of his being with his beloved. He gives the same prudent
advice to the Carthusians of Mont Dieu: "Love to be devoutly employed
within in charity contemplating the truth, but when necessity calls or duty
draws do most readily lend, but not give, yourselves without for the truth of
fulfilling charity."—no. 6, trans. Shewring, p. 15.

19. Cf. 1 Cor 7:31.

as he is, but every soul that has merited the name of Bride shall be
as he is.[20] The kiss will also know its plenitude when, kiss to kiss
and embrace to embrace, full and abiding fruition shall be attained.
Then nevermore shall anyone stir up the Bride nor make her to
awake, until she please; and never again will she please.

99. Meanwhile amid the anguish of this life, as a help in her
labors and a comfort in her time of waiting, a paradise is set out
for the Bride's soul and, for her conscience, a little flowery bed
where she finds not that eternal kiss and perfect union, but a certain
remote imitation of that kiss and perfection, and a certain likeness
of that union and likeness. For by the action of the Holy Spirit,
man's spirit and the sense of enlightened love sometimes fleetingly
attain to it. Then that something, whatever it is—something loved
rather than thought, and tasted rather than understood—grows
sweet and ravishes the lover. And for a moment, for an hour, this
affects him and shapes his efforts until it seems to him that no longer
in hope but in quasi-reality he sees with his eyes, and holds and
handles with his hands, by a sort of evidence of experimental faith,
the very substance of things to be hoped for of the Word of life.[21]

100. Yes, O Father, this is the consolation you give your children,
as you promised: "I will not leave you orphans; I go away, and I
am coming to you."[22] For you bow your heavens and come down[23]
in favor of your children of hope, bound in the prison of this exile;
and you dwell and move among them.[24] And answering to their
faith, which you first placed in their hearts, little by little you
bestow your grace, grace for grace.[25] Thanks to its operation they
conform to it their spirit and their life; and there is brought about
that likeness which is immediately accompanied by fruition. O
good Father, good Lord, good in whatsoever you are, you show
and manifest yourself to be the Good, as you are, in order to arouse

20. Cf. 1 Jn 3:2.   21. Cf. Heb 11:1; 1 Jn 1:1.
22. Cf. Jn 14:18.   23. Ps 17:10; 143:5.
24. Cf. 2 Cor 6:16.   25. Cf. Jn 1:16.

the love of your children. And since power to heal our diseases ever goes forth from you,[26] you affect them by a sort of contact or experience of your goodness and make them good by something of yourself. Thus you who are good are loved by those who are good; and you yourself are your love in them, mercifully and sweetly affecting them by something of yourself and most rightly, most justly and most wisely loving yourself by something of them. For that which tastes you is not alien from you, and that which grasps you is not far from you—if it does grasp you, when no place (sensible or intelligible) holds you, and no sense (using the body as instrument or the reason as means of comprehension) grasps you. But the welcoming breast of love, opening yet wider to meet your magnitude, while it loves you or aspires to love you in all your greatness, grasps the ungraspable and comprehends the incomprehensible. But what am I saying? "It grasps"? Nay rather, it is very Love (and you are Love) that grasps—it is your Holy Spirit, O Father, who proceeds from you and from the Son, with whom you and the Son are one.[27] When the spirit of man deserves to be drawn to him, spirit to Spirit, love to Love, then human love becomes in a certain manner divine; from then on, when man loves God, man is at work, but it is God who works. Not Paul, but the grace of God with him.[28]

101. The Bride says therefore, "Our little bed is flowery." She offers the Bridegroom what she desires to receive from him. This offering is a devout prayer, for love breaks out anew when it recalls the object it loves exceedingly, and the great desire aroused in one who remembers is a loving prayer. This remembrance is nothing else than the invitation by which the Bride's holy conscience summons her Confidant within her. She already possesses the flowers of the little flowery bed, that is, the charm of holy virtues given by the Bridegroom in approbation of her good will; but she

26. Cf. Lk 6:19.   27. Cf. Jn 15:26; 10:30.   28. Cf. 1 Cor 15:10.

I

cannot derive enjoyment from her fondness for them unless the Bridegroom is present to her and she—in him—to herself. And so she offers the little flowery bed and invites him to it. Begging with tears for repose, in peace in the selfsame she desires rest.[29] By the illuminating grace of the Bridegroom's constant presence, she wishes to have her memory fixed and firmly directed upon God and her understanding illuminated by him; she seeks that love of him which surpasses knowledge;[30] and, in the accomplishment of virtues, the constant sweetness of the attractions of grace.

102. "Our little bed is flowery." Just as a flower strongly tends to mature and to yield fruit, so a will that is good strongly tends to love. This is the Bride's goal; to attain it, she travails and is made uneasy. She wishes for love, she desires fruition, not with ambition of will but with poise of soul; this is how she greatly longs for the little flowery bed. For it is not in the tendency of the soul seeking God—where likeness to him must be brought about—that gratuitous fruition of God can exist.

103. This is why she says "our little bed." When it is "ours," she says, common to me and to you, it will breathe forth holy delights and glow with mutual love. But as long as it remains "mine," the little bed in which by night I seek him whom I love and find him not,[31] it has no hint of flowers or perfumes, little charm and never a vestige of joy; it is a little bed of night and not of day; its whole surface is cold, and woe to him who lies in it alone, for there will be no one to warm him.[32] This is why it is not "my" little bed, but "our" little flowery bed.

104. A while ago she had some experience of love for the Bridegroom, and now she sighs after the bed. For an hour she tasted that which is imperfect, and now she desires repose and rest in that which is perfect. For in contemplation of the highest Good, through the natural attraction of that same Good, whatever delights the

29. Cf. Ps 4:9.   30. Cf. Eph 3:19.
31. Cf. Song 3:1.   32. Cf. Eccles 4:10 f.

lover is wont to appear, to the believer, immediately obtainable; and in the light of God's countenance, just as there can never be love without its object, so there can never be knowledge without hope.

105. Now come these words: "The beams of our houses are cedars." Not only the little bed, she says, but our houses too are averse to solitude. Woe then to the person who dwells alone, be it in the little bed or in the house. The Bride possesses not merely one house; count the number of virtues she possesses, for she has the same number of houses to dwell in and to dwell in with her Bridegroom. The houses of the Bride are holy virtues, concerning which we read in the psalm: "In her (that is, in the Bride's) houses, God shall be known, when he (the Bridegroom) shall protect her."[33] The Bridegroom is indeed known in the Bride's houses when they are illuminated by the grace of his presence—a presence welcome, accepted and pleasing in her sight. For the chastity motivated by charity is one thing; that caused merely by continence is another. Each and every one of the virtues is one thing merely in the appetite of the will, by the judgment of reason, and another thing in the loving impulse of vivifying grace.

As long as their houses (the houses of virtues) continue common to both Bridegroom and Bride, they retain their incomparable defense, the "beams of cedar," and their interior adornment, the "rafters of cypresses." In the houses of virtues, the beams of incorruptible cedar are faith and the hope of eternity; beneath the roof of God's protection, they are raised toward heaven by the strength of a right intention. The rafters of cypresses by their beautiful workmanship and strong fragrance signify the interior adornment of carefulness to preserve the unity of the Spirit. This unity, in the charity of God, is the mutual charity of the children of the Bridegroom for one another, in that they love one another and uphold one another, as, in the rafters, timbers are braced by other timbers to achieve the interior adornment and likewise the

33. Cf. Ps 47:4.

interior defenses—so that nothing may enter surreptitiously or thrust itself in to disturb the dwellers in the house, since one single charity disposes them for mutual giving and receiving.

Certain unbelievers seem, it is true, to possess the virtues of the soul; but no virtue can be proven such if it is not lifted toward God by faith and hope, and if it does not belong within the family unity of the Church's devotion. For the natural charm of the virtues seems to invite or attract all men; but without God's help, love of these same virtues is felt by few, and their truth impresses none. Therefore, as has been said, even those who are outside sometimes appear to have certain virtues as springs of action, to want them and even to love them, for one of their spokesmen says men can be called good only if for love of virtue they forbear to sin.[34] But when Christ is our wisdom, he is our every virtue as well, all the plenitude of virtue being contained in wisdom. And any given virtue is no virtue unless it enables its possessor to savor him who is the Wisdom of all virtues. As true and solid virtue is found in him (not merely zeal for labor or ambition of will, but the soul's inclination and the habit of a well-disposed mind), so when love is directed toward him, it is true and living. Thus through the understanding or the experience of love, he who is loved becomes present to the lover; and then the little bed is not only ours but flowery.

106. Everything then that the Bride said to the Bridegroom about the little flowery bed and the houses with their beams and rafters, is nothing else than an invitation by which the devout conscience calls God, her Confidant, into her heart. Or put it this way, that under the beams of faith and hope, that is, in the common life of the faithful, the Bride seeks the flowery bed; and under the rafters of life in society, she seeks a safe mansion for a fixed abode, where she may protect with greater secrecy the transactions of mutual

---

34. The reference here is to Horace, Book 1, Letter 16, line 52; trans. E. Wickham, *Horace for English Readers* (London: Oxford Univ. Press, 1930), p. 300.

fruition and love between herself and the Bridegroom. But fruition and love seek a more suitable place, one more charming for their repose, more secret for their enjoyment, safer for their abode. This place is charity itself, from a pure heart and a good conscience and faith unfeigned;[35] it is the heart which—in the desert or in the midst of the throng—is solitary in God.

35. Cf. 1 Tim 1:5.

I am the Flower of the field
    and the Lily of the valleys.
As the lily among the thorns,
So is my love among the daughters.

As the apple tree among the trees of the woods,
So is my Beloved among the sons.

I sat down under his shadow, whom I desired:
And his fruit was sweet to my palate.[1]

AFTER this follows: "I am the Flower of the field and the Lily of the valleys." The Spirit of wisdom, before enriching a man, is wont to make him poor of spirit; and before uplifting him, to humble him, that he may support the height of true perfection upon the foundation of true humility. But the height of the cellar of wine, into which the Bridegroom is preparing to bring the Bride, will not admit any other heights than that of which it is said, "the greater you are, the more you must humble yourself in all things."[2] For as all strength is made perfect in weakness,[3] so all justice is made perfect in humility. That is why when the Lord was about to be baptized in the Jordan he said to John: "Let it be so now: for so it becomes us to fulfill all justice."[4] Not so much to

1. Song 2:1ff.   2. Sir 3:20.
3. Cf. 2 Cor 12:9.   4. Mt 3:15.

prove the fulfillment of justice in the Bride as to approve the virtue of humility, the Bridegroom says therefore: "I am the Flower of the field and the Lily of the valleys. As the lily among the thorns, so is my love among the daughters." As if he said: If you aspire to the fullness of fruition, labor and strive to possess the fullness of my likeness, in other words, the virtue of perfect humility in all its perfection; for this is the virtue of which I, the Flower of the field and the Lily of the valleys, am your exemplar.

108. The flower of the field and the lily of the valley differ notably one from the other. Of course there is one variety of humility proper to the fields and plains; from this no bearer of the Christian name can hold himself excused. It is common to all men, merely in accordance with the natural judgment of reason, namely that everyone should be submissive to a person who is greater than he and not prefer himself to an equal.

But there is a more sublime humility which looks for the reward of perfection; it consists in being submissive to one's inferior and preferring one's equal to oneself for God's sake, not merely by the judgment of reason, but by impulse of conscience. This is the lily of the valley, of deep hearts, of holy souls, of perfect men, who anticipate one another with honor[5] and regard each other mutually as superiors.[6] Adjacent mountains are divided by the lofty walls of the valley between them and united by its depth. No doubt the Apostle speaks of souls like these when he says: "There are diversities of gifts or graces, but the same Spirit."[7] And the Psalmist speaks of them when he says: "You send forth springs in the vales."[8] And elsewhere: "The vales shall abound with corn."[9] In the lofty heights of their respective merits and the sublimity of their respective sanctity, these perfect men are differentiated; but in the depths

5. Cf. Rom 12:10.

6. The Rule of St Benedict according to which William lived has a chapter which calls upon the brethren to obey each other. *St Benedict's Rule for Monasteries*, ch. 71: "That the Brethern Should Obey Each Other."

7. Cf. 1 Cor 12:4.   8. Ps 103:10.   9. Ps 64:14.

of their consciences, where they humble themselves, the devout judgment of charity unites them. The more sublime the heights of charity in these souls, the deeper will the valley of their humility prove to be.

Here lily resembles Lily; that is, the copy is conformed and like to the exemplar of the sacred humility in Christ. For the ordinary man's humility is one thing, when in view of his human condition and his self-knowledge, he holds himself worthless in the sight of God and his neighbor; but very different is the humility of a God-man, abasing himself, by his own will, to the lowest degree of human condition in order to raise man up. For in the Mediator between God and man,[10] this condescension toward man, proceeding from the one and only source of Goodness, is rather humiliation than humility. This is why the Apostle says, "He humbled himself."[11] In man, however, self-knowledge is always humility; in him who wishes it not, it is shame he cannot escape; but in him who wishes it, it is virtue he yearns for.

109. The man Christ, then, appeared as a Flower of the field, the exemplar of humility for all men, of whom it is written that he was subject to his parents.[12] As sharing in the liability to pay tribute, he did not refuse to be on an equal footing with Peter for both the payment and the amount due. When the collectors asked for tribute to the earthly empire, he said to him: "Go to the sea and cast in a hook, and open the mouth of the first fish that comes

10. *Infra*, no. 159. William develops further the foundation of Christ's mediatorial role. William was very conscious of Christ as the mediator. In his very first work, *On the Nature and Dignity of Love*, he spoke of this at length. See esp. chs. 9ff. (trans. Webb and Walker, pp. 44ff.): "At the end of every prayer we may say 'through Jesus Christ our Lord,' because we direct all prayer and sacrifice to God through him as through our mediator, and because whatever we hope for from the Father we ask to be poured into the body through that mouth which is Christ."—*loc. cit.*

11. Phil 2:8. St Bernard speaks more fully of the humility and humiliation of the God-man in his commentary on the Song of Songs. Cf. Sermon 42.

12. Cf. Lk 2:51.

up, and you will find a stater. Give it to them for me and for you."[13]

110. Christ was also a Lily of the valleys, when being man and preferring other men to himself, of his own will he died for the wicked that they might live; or again when, being the God-man, he freely submitted himself to evil men and was judged by them unjustly. It follows, he says, that both the flat level of an ordinary life and the profession of a higher life find in me patterns of humility to imitate. For I appeared to some as a Flower of the field, to others as a Lily standing taller than other flowers, that I might be a model of perfection; though I was by nature God, I did not consider being equal to God a thing to be clung to, but emptied myself, being made like unto men and appearing in the form of men.[14] As for you [my Bride] intent on him who is fair, so that by him you yourself may be made fair, you have experienced in yourself by the sense of love what you experienced in me by the sense of faith. Planted together with the Lily, you have become like the Lily; you have not been turned away from the straight path of imitation of me either by womanish weakness, conveyed by the term "daughters," or by the sharp point of thorns, that is, the malice of those who dwell with you. For to lead a good life in the midst of evil men is already a high summit of perfection.

We must be aware, however, that man's supreme example of humility comes from Christ; although humility is one thing in Christ and another in the Christian. In any mere man, no doubt, it is true humility to judge oneself in accordance with reality, and by self-knowledge to become worthless in one's own eyes. Now Jesus Christ, who is the Truth, even though he surpassed other men in humility by his actions and teachings, could not judge himself save in accordance with reality. For since he was both God and man, as man he was so worthy of God that there was nothing in him by which he could become worthless in his own eyes. For him, therefore, humility lay not in judgment but in deeds; and he humbled

13. Mt 17:26.   14. Cf. Phil 2:7.

himself not only by inculcating humility, but by surpassing all men in doing and enduring the things that were humblest and most unworthy of his majesty.

111. The Bridegroom is therefore the Flower of the field and the Lily of the valleys; the Bride, for her part, is as the lily. So the Bride, embracing the humility of imitation and devout likeness but fearing the lofty summits of equality with her Beloved, does not refuse likeness to the lily, which is humble but unfruitful. But she compares the Bridegroom to the lofty, fruit-laiden apple tree, affording her protecting shadow and life-giving fruit, and she says: "As the apple tree among the trees of the wood, so is my Beloved among the sons. I sat under his shadow, whom I desired: and his fruit was sweet to my palate."

112. Man is never to be compared with God—not even in this likeness of humility. The power of the omnipotent Trinity is incomparable, its majesty inscrutable, its virtue inestimable, its wisdom inconceivable; and so, coming into the world, God's weakness was found stronger than all men, his foolishness wiser and his humility more sublime.[15] This is why the Lord says, speaking of John, "Among those born of women there has not risen a greater than John the Baptist"[16]—greater, that is, in humility. Yet he who is the lesser—that is, humbler—in the kingdom of heaven, is greater than he.[17] In what? In humility. In the kingdom of heaven, that is, in the Church, John's humility shone forth in its greatness. But greater in the Church than John did he appear who, although he was greater than all the rest, showed himself as the least and in the world appeared humbler than all the humble, inasmuch as he descended from on high to the depths of our earth.

The Bride, in view of the teaching she received from the Bridegroom and the experience she derived from temptations, is intent on imitation of him but afraid of equality with him; therefore under the figure of the lofty apple tree she calls up the picture of the

15. Cf. 1 Cor 1:25.   16. Mt 11:11.   17. *Ibid.*

Lord's repose with his disciples at the banquet in the Pharisee's house, herself entering in the guise of the sinful woman, and the Lord justifying her.[18] All this story of evangelical tenderness she transposes in her own favor, when she says: As the apple tree, laden with fruit among the barren trees of the woods, enhances them with its beauty, gladdens them with its fragrance and honors them with its fruit, so my Beloved, reposing among the sons of tender affection and virile strength, namely the Apostles, enlightens them by his virtues, strengthens them by his example, confirms them by his works and gladdens them by his doctrine. Under the shadow of his defense, when the Pharisee condemned me, I anxiously desired to be protected and hidden; but when I heard from his lips the verdict for those who love the Lord, I sat the more securely. For he said: "Her sins, many as they are, shall be forgiven her, because she has loved much."[19]

113. "And his fruit was sweet to my palate." As if she said: The taste of his love satisfies my desire with good things, at the moment when the fullness of his pardon gladdens my conscience by the words: "Your faith has saved you; go in peace."[20] I desired, when I went about impelled by faith and hope; I sat, when I rested in him through love of the Spirit; and his fruit was sweet to my palate, when by the power of enlightened love I began to taste the sweet experience of his sweetness.

18. Cf. Lk 7:36f.   19. Lk 7:47.   20. Lk 7:50.

STANZA 10

The King brought me into the cellar of wine;
He set in order charity in me.

Stay me up with flowers,
Compass me about with apples:
Because I languish with love.[1]

AFTER this follows: "The King brought me into the cellar of wine." For now she who earlier went forth from the storerooms in mature piety[2] and sought anxiously for contemplation,[3] has been tried in all things,[4] profoundly purified[5] and fitly humbled.[6] She is beginning to enter into the place of the wonderful tabernacle, even to the house of God,[7] that she may now recline at table and have fruition of what she was wont to desire so impatiently when she said: "Show me, O you whom my soul loves, where you feed, where you have your couch in the midday."

115. For as we have said already, it is of these places that the prophet declares: "The riches of salvation are wisdom and knowledge."[8] In knowledge, that is, in the storerooms, reason and understanding are fed; in wisdom, which is the cellar of wine, are fed love and affection. The riches of the storerooms are known; the

1. Song 2:4f.
2. Cf. *supra*, nos. 26, 30ff.
3. Cf. *supra*, nos. 35ff.
4. Cf. *supra*, nos. 29, 62ff.
5. Cf. *supra*, nos. 69ff.
6. Cf. *supra*, nos. 107ff.
7. Cf. Ps 41:5.
8. Is 33:6.

riches of the cellar of wine are tasted. In the storerooms, one must labor diligently to understand; in the cellar of wine, one has but to rejoice in experiencing fruition. The things which appertain to knowledge are not the property of all, but are laboriously brought in from without, as it were, by those engaged in learning. But the things which appertain to wisdom, like possessions of nature, are discovered within and increased freely without labor even by the guileless sons of God, who think of the Lord in goodness and seek God in simplicity of heart.[9] The cellar of wine, indeed, is a certain secret of God's wisdom; it is the state of the soul that is more fully drawn to cleave to God. This state may be likened to the temple of God, in that it is separated from heavenly things, that is, from the holy of holies, only by the veil of this mortal life.[10] It has a sure and familiar communion with heavenly things according to the measure of the soul's progress and the gift of illuminating grace. And here is the flowery bed, the bed of delights, which the Bride was seeking a little while before;[11] she will take possession of it not under the cedar beams of faith and hope,[12] but in the fullness of charity, which is the cellar of wine.

116. For charity, or a good conscience in its perfection, is the cellar of wine; and the wine of this cellar is joy in the Holy Spirit. In the cellar of wine, therefore, nothing is found but wine. Whatever enters there, whatever is brought in, either is wine or becomes wine, because the fire of the love of God wholly claims and consumes it and, in the manner of the element of fire, converts it into its own substance, since to him that loves God all things work together unto good.[13]

9. Cf. Wis 1:1.

10. This passage is found almost verbatim in William's *Letter to the Carthusians of Mont Dieu,* no. 65, trans. Shewring, pp. 111f.

11. Cf. *supra,* nos. 95ff.

12. Cf. *supra,* nos. 105f. In this paragraph William has resumed the whole development of his *Exposition* up to this point.

13. Cf. Rom 8:28.

117. There, thanks to the great quantity of wine, the plenty of God's house and the torrent of pleasure,[14] charity in such wise grows impetuous, overflows in its excesses and rejoices over what it longs for, that very often it seems to abandon order, unless it is set in order anew by the King. Thus Paul wished to be anathema from Christ for his brethren,[15] and Moses asked that he might be struck out of the book of life unless the people of God were forgiven their heinous sin.[16] The joy of a conscience which, by charity, is rendered good in the sight of God, is not diminished but rather increased if it sometimes feels the sadness, suffering and sorrow of others. For when the joy of the Lord is established in a good conscience, it is not interrupted by the incursion of any earthly sadness or obscured by any vain joyousness but continues faithfully and firmly in its steady course, always and everywhere tranquil, nor does it undergo change even though it lends itself to many things. Here the disturbance of men and the contradiction of tongues effect nothing.[17] We are far from vain joyousness and from all sadness, for here the old man has been completely mortified, and all that lives on the taste of the highest Good is the sense of sweetness and love of godliness. We are far from the vain and trivial mirth that is wont to insinuate itself from without, flushing the face without filling the heart and coloring the skin without penetrating the inner depths. For these are the joys of the world which ravage the soul, causing it to dwell on mental images of vain pleasures. After robbing the mind of whatever strength or virtue it possessed, they disappear and pass away, doing more harm than any kind of sadness.

But the joy of the Lord is an austere thing. The gravity it requires is exemplified in those who rejoice and exult not only when they hear that their names are written in heaven [18] and that their reward is very great,[19] but also when they fall into divers temptations and,

---

14. Cf. Ps 35:9.

16. Cf. Ex 32:32.

18. Cf. Lk 10:20.

15. Cf. Rom 9:3.

17. Cf. Ps 30:21.

19. Cf. Lk 6:23.

for the sake of the God they love, the world hates them, and men cast them out and reproach their name as evil.[20] In truth the joy which comes from without quickly departs again, but the holy conscience which does not rejoice in what is extraneous to itself rejoices always since it has the source of its joy within.

118. For joy is the family possession and sure felicity of the good conscience of which the prophet says, where he praises the blessed man who fears the Lord: "Glory and wealth shall be in his house."[21] And the Apostle says: "Our glory is this, the testimony of our conscience."[22] But is not a good conscience one that takes pleasure in the love of God and is true to itself in faithful service of his love? This joy is not in laughter of the lips but in jubilation of the heart; for he who rejoices thus, no matter what misfortune or adversity befalls him, is always cheerful and unconcerned, thanks to his good conscience, surmounting all happenings by turning upward to God. Assuredly joy is the undisturbed fruition of the object loved.

119. For this reason, from the mode or quality of love follows the mode or quality of joy, and truer joy is wont to be produced when the object of love is truer. The love of God therefore has its own proper joy, joy in the Holy Spirit, which no one takes from the lover[23] because it is his—because it is the sure possession of his conscience. And this is the wine of the cellar of wine. The Apostle Paul was inebriated with this wine when he said: "Who shall separate us from the charity of God? Shall tribulation? Or distress? Or persecution? Or famine? Or nakedness? Or danger? Or the sword? For I am sure that neither death nor life, nor angels, nor principalities, nor powers, nor virtues, nor things present, nor things to come, nor might, nor height, nor depth, nor any other creature shall be able to separate us from the charity of God which is in Christ Jesus our Lord."[24] And the Psalmist says: "My chalice which inebriates me, how goodly is it!"[25] This indeed is the wine

---

20. Cf. Lk 6:22.
22. 2 Cor 1:12.
24. Cf. Rom 8:35ff.

21. Ps 111:3.
23. Cf. Jn 16:22.
25. Ps 22:5.

already scented with the strength of that which Jesus drinks new with his disciples in the kingdom of his Father;[26] the wine which the prophet describes as creating virgins;[27] the wine, as the psalmist said, of sorrow,[28] or the wine that gladdens the heart of man.[29] Truly a man's sorrow caused by desire and his gladness due to fruition seem to be in a certain manner contrary the one to the other; but nevertheless both belong to the cellar of wine and to a good conscience, and they flow from the same spring of love.

120. The Bride therefore is led into the house of wine, into the joy of her Lord and Bridegroom; but at the first experiences of this blessing, impatient of measure and reason, from an abundance of wine she abandons order and yields to the inebriation of exceeding fervor and the languor of human weakness, fainting after God's salvation.[30] For loving and loving much, if she were not inordinate in this very love, if she loved prudently, temperately, with fortitude and justice, she would not languish. For what causes languor in bodies if not disordered humors? Indeed it is the natural order of holy love that by the help of prudence we should understand and be wise, but be wise according to sobriety,[31] which is temperance; and, by the help of fortitude, do the things we have understood, but in accordance with justice. For when prudence is not wise according to sobriety, fortitude strives to do more than justice allows; then everything abandons order and languor sets in. Now when love has abandoned order, it makes all else do the same; and pursuing its goal inordinately, it does not attain it, but faints and languishes. Sometimes indeed love strives more impetuously than is right and, insofar as it is aware of its own purity, presumes to be its own law and its own order, being unwilling that anyone should set it in order. But when the King sets it in order and rules it, even the sick man's languor is ordered in such wise that no matter how

26. Cf. Mt 26:29; Mk 14:25.
28. Cf. Ps 59:5.
30. Cf. Ps 118:81.

27. Cf. Zech 9:17.
29. Cf. Ps 103:15.
31. Cf. Rom 12:3.

he is agitated and overwhelmed, all the holy discipline of his sickness and of the duress of his cure contain more joy than sadness. For this joy and that grief, his devout affection due to fruition and his anxious longing caused by desire, exercise a mutual attraction and correspond like harmonious antitheses. He who languishes, therefore, does not wish to be cured; he who grieves does not wish to be comforted. In fact he rejoices that he is fainting in love, for he feels that this love is making progress by his very failure. And when to some extent he has tasted that the Lord is sweet,[32] he begins to think of the Lord in goodness,[33] to feel somewhat the highest Good, to admire and contemplate the supreme Beauty. Now in part he understands[34] with his intelligence the beatitude of fruition and the joy of incorruptibility and immutability.

121. He seeks with all his might to escape to the state of blessedness; but as he cannot, being a man corruptible and mutable, he is seized with disgust for the corruption of his mortal life. And since it is said to him: "Man shall not see me and live,"[35] he conceives a violent hatred of his own life, whatever its form, which delays or impedes the life of seeing God. He is eager then to die, but that is forbidden him; to die for Christ, but that is not granted him; to die in Christ, but that is deferred. He makes ready to live in Christ, and his intelligence is blinded; to attend upon God, but his ferment of mind will not allow him; to set to work, but there is no place for his work. He wishes to spend, but has not the wherewithal; to be weighed out and to be spent, and finds no opportunity. He says, he cries aloud: "Lord, what will you have me do?"[36]—and no answer is vouchsafed him. "What will you have me to become?"—and he is left to his own devices. For he wishes to perform just deeds by the exercise of his own reason, and he fails in making distinctions. He wishes to become just by the exercise of his own

32. Cf. Ps 33:9.   33. Cf. Wis 1:1.   34. Cf. 1 Cor 13:9.
35. Ex 33:20.   36. Acts 9:6.

K

affection, and he cannot without the aid of God. The sick man is prescribed his medicine and does not listen. Love is taught its law and does not accept it. He who has abandoned order is shown what order is and pays no heed. Indeed he is commanded to love the Lord his God with his whole heart and with his whole soul and with all his mind and with all his strength, and his neighbor as himself.[37] But wherever the impetuosity of love gains the upper hand, he knows not, at one moment, if he loves either himself or his neighbor for the love of God; at the next moment, if he loves either God or his neighbor for the love of self; and again, if he loves either God or himself for the love of neighbor. Yet true love, either of self or of one's neighbor, if it proceeds in its proper order and measure, is nothing else but love of God. This is the languor of the Bride who languishes for love. This is love strong as death. This is jealousy hard as hell.[38] This is the inebriation caused by the plenty of God's house and the torrent of his pleasure.[39]

122. Another sort of languor may be found in the Bride in her thoughts of the Bridegroom. This happens by the vice of a conscience sometimes unheeded; when memory is defiled, then understanding grows dull and love languishes. For it is these three faculties—memory, understanding and love—which, according as they are better or worse, greater or lesser, form our thought of God. If then memory, when it is considering God, flits now in one direction and now in another, and if it is remiss, negligent or unfaithful, understanding is consequently null, feeble or insignificant and prone to error. Moreover love is null or corrupt, to wit, when God is thought of for any reason but that he should be loved, or when he is loved for any reason but his own sake.

But if memory, in the thought of faith, burns to understand, never setting a limit here but striving for love through understanding, then he who loves and tends towards God often finds at

37. Cf. Mt 22:37ff.; Lk 10:27.   38. Cf. Song 8:6.   39. Cf. Ps 35:9.

hand the blessed experience he seeks, when understanding passes into love or love into understanding, according to the grace of the Giver and the zeal or godliness of him who receives. For when understanding sees but fails to penetrate something, as increased knowledge adds sorrow,[40] so increased wisdom increases love: then understanding rejoices to see and languishes with desire to penetrate deeper, without fully resting in what it receives, which is in part,[41] while it eagerly pursues what it has not yet received, which is perfect. For what is loved must be understood. What is understood must be thought. For unless what is loved is found at hand by the lover through his memory and becomes known through his understanding, love itself decays and languishes. This occurs especially in those things the fruition of which is prepared for love through memory and understanding alone—as in things rational, still more in things spiritual and most of all in things divine.

Therefore the soul possessed by love for its heavenly country and for God the Father, is extremely vexed that its memory should journey in strange places and its understanding attend to strange occupations. When love cannot perfectly free itself therefrom, having been unwillingly entangled in a certain will of the flesh, it languishes in its isolation and suffers what the prophet refers to when he says: "The Lord lives, whose fire is in Sion and his furnace in Jerusalem."[42] Fire of its nature always rushes upward, and when it is enclosed inside a furnace, in its isolation it burns all the more for being forcibly detained within barriers. Thus the torrent which has been detained rushes forth the more impetuously; the fire which has been shut up burns more forcibly; the Bride's love, which has been held in check, cannot be restrained. When this love of hers, being detained by the bond of the flesh, cannot wholly escape to that region whither it is wholly drawn, it is impatient of law and seizes, like fire, upon everything in reach: her loving soul pours

40. Cf. Eccles 1:18.   41. Cf. 1 Cor 13:9.   42. Is 31:9.

itself out wholly upon her neighbor, hoping it may thus perchance deserve to ascend by a shorter path, in greater purity, to God.

123. For this reason the Bride, turning to the young maidens, the daughters of Jerusalem, the daughters of heavenly peace, companions of her desire and sharers of her love, says: "Stay me up with flowers, compass me about with apples, because I languish with love."

For she cannot but love goodness in others, since it serves as the chief comfort of her own inner grief. Anyone who truly loves God, loves and embraces divine love wherever he finds it. When he considers its form in his neighbor, it often pleases him more than in himself. This is because, seeing no conscience but his own, he sees in himself both what appears to men and what is concealed from them. But in his neighbor he sees only what appears—to wit, certain fruits of the Spirit and of love—whereby he divines and loves in him the inner love which he does not see. In himself he sees both what he lacks and what he possesses; but as to his neighbor, he can judge only by what he sees in him. Moreover, he censures his own doings in strict justice, but he interprets all his neighbor's doings in a good sense out of benevolent charity. Some slight good therefore in his neighbor, whose mixed interior state he does not see, often pleases him more than some great good in himself, from the mixed quality whereof he is the only one to suffer. Another man who is a beginner pleases him more than himself, although he is more advanced; and another's advanced state pleases him more than his own perfection. As a result, by the benevolence of his fraternal charity he enjoys in his neighbor what he cannot enjoy in himself, even when it is present in him and to a higher degree than in his neighbor. For as we have said, in his neighbor, whose conscience is hidden from him, only the appearance of good is revealed, and this he embraces as if it were in himself, and with fraternal love he wishes his neighbor joy. In himself, however, what is offensive weighs so much more on his conscience that even if something pleasing should chance to be there, it would not dare to appear before the face of one who judges himself with such severity. When therefore the very Author of charity has set in order the Bride's charity, she conceives a disgust for her own faults. Then she goes forth completely and gives herself up to wishing others joy in their progress. As we have said, she regards others' beginnings as better than her own end, and others' progress as better than her own perfection.

124. By the flowers, which contain the hope of fruit, is certainly denoted the fair hope of beginners; but by the apples, the fruit of the perfect. By the flowers the Bride is stayed up that she may experience delights. By the apples she is compassed about that she may exercise virtue. And the flowers of the new creature in Christ[43] smell sweeter to her in beginners than do the fruits of her own perfection in herself. The fruits of others' justice smell sweeter than does the awareness of any sanctity of her own. In their flowers she finds an incitement to virtue; in their fruit, a confirmation of it.

125. But again, according to outward appearances, the quality of youthful holiness lays claim to a certain grace in learning the way of godliness; and aged holiness, because the firmness of its fidelity is surer, claims reverence. Youthfulness, indeed, has a cheerful disposition, adaptable for all things. Like soft wax, it readily receives whatever impression is made on it and retains that impression well-formed, especially when something natural, that is, something in the order of virtue, is imprinted on it. And as virtue adds beauty to age, so the flower of age itself gives greater grace to virtue. Age likewise, when it is advanced in what is good, commends itself to every conscience possessed of some love of good. Its earlier life causes it to be praised for the past; its proven virtue removes all suspicion of inconstancy for the future; and well-worn old age, by the very law of nature, wins itself reverence. And as in youth virtue appears more pleasing, so in old age it appears surer and more beautiful, as if on its proper throne.

126. The Bride therefore is stayed up by the flowers of the young,

43. Cf. 2 Cor 5:17; Gal 6:15.

but compassed about by the apples of the old. Delighted with the flowers and strengthened by the fruit, she finds comfort for her own weakness in the progress of young and old. And when a man of God accounts his neighbor better than himself, he not only loves him as himself, but also honors him more than himself.

127. For this is the order of charity and the rightful term of languishing love. First, indeed, the Lord God is loved with a man's whole heart, that he may be constantly thought of with the devout memory; with his whole soul, that his life may always be in him and for him; with man's whole strength, that all his powers may be faithfully spent in the work of serving him; with his whole mind, that he may be loved perfectly and with understanding. Next, after the love of God, a covenant of nature and good will with every man is needful; but for himself and for his neighbor as himself, he must have the affection of religious love. Our neighbor must be whoever is of the household of faith.[44] And among our neighbors let that man be more loved, as being nearer to us, who by the merit of his life and love of godliness is found to be more united to God, in whom he is our neighbor and in whom he is loved.

128. In the same way, one who is God's beloved and God's lover loves himself well and in right order if he cares for his flesh not according to its desires but for the sake of the spirit, and if he shows charity to his spirit in the Holy Spirit for God's sake. For we do not love for the body's sake, yet we cannot live without the body. But we live that we may cleave to God by our spirit and that, by loving him in godliness and sincerity, we may live soberly with respect to ourself, justly with respect to our neighbor and godly with respect to God and, by so living, may deserve to live hereafter blessedly and eternally in God. Therefore, according to the Apostle who said: "no man ever hates his own flesh,"[45] it suffices not to hate the body, although give it care we must, short of servitude to it. To the spirit, however, a man must show charity and do honor, even to the point

44. Cf. Gal 6:10.   45. Eph 5:29.

of complete servitude on the part of the body. For a certain care by the spirit is owed to the body that the body may live, but unstinted service by the body is owed to the spirit that the spirit may wax strong; and service by both is owed to God that the whole man may serve God.[46] Thus he whose charity is well-ordered loves the Lord his God, and himself in him, and his neighbor as himself, with a love of the same quality and intensity. For even if perchance the perfection of charity is greater in him than in his neighbor, he desires that it should be as great in his neighbor as that which he cherishes in himself. But if he finds or accounts his neighbor's charity greater, he enjoys him in God the more sweetly and, as we have said, honors him more than himself.

129. This it is, therefore, for a man to love God as the Lord his God, and to love himself aright and his neighbor as himself. This is the order of charity ordained by the law of the Spirit of life, proclaimed by the Word of God in the Holy Spirit; written by the finger of God in the heart of him who loves according to right order, and formed by God in a certain manner in man's natural reason. Hence it is that the judgment of reason discerns this order and the instinct of a good will approves it; but without the breath of the grace of the Holy Spirit, the good soul's affection possesses it not.

130. First therefore the Bride is brought into the cellar of wine, and then charity is set in order in her. In truth when she first enters, because she still needs to be set in order and is still inebriated, she strives to do more than she can and endeavors to accomplish, as if by one single exertion of love, whatever God wills. But fainting after God's salvation,[47] she languishes until, after additional progress and blessed advance, the King sets in order charity in her, and she moreover begins to will what God wills. And then, by this conformity of will, she becomes one spirit with God.[48] A moment ago,

46. William gives similar, although perhaps somewhat more severe, advice to the Carthusians of Mont Dieu in his *Letter*, no. 18, trans. Shewring, pp. 37f.
47. Cf. Ps 118:81, 123. 48. Cf. 1 Cor 6:17.

her spirit was inebriated, and now it becomes sober. It was languishing and is now sound. It was impetuous and now submits to order. In its inebriation, it hastens to slumber; languishing, it seeks the flowery bed; impetuous, it reaches out to be embraced. And thus the union of Bridegroom and Bride is most delightful.

131. O God, you who are charity, Holy Spirit, Love of the Father and the Son, and substantial Will, dwell within us and set us in order that your will may be done in us. May your will become our will, that being ready to do the will of the Lord our God, we may find his law and his order in the midst of our heart. Enlighten the eyes of our heart,[49] that we may contemplate with them the immutable light of your truth until it regulates the order of our changeableness and our changeable and wavering will. May your Bride—that is to say, our soul—by loving you, understand in your very love what she must do with herself. Nay rather, do you who dwell in her as God, you who are yourself your love in her, bring it to pass in her that she shall love you through yourself, O you who are her Love; and may you yourself, in her, love yourself through her. And in her, may you do with her and set all things in order, according to yourself.

This is why you said of old to your servant Moses: "See that you make all things according to the pattern that was shown you on the mount."[50] On the mount, of a truth, the pattern of life and sanctity was shown to Moses when, in the height of the most exalted contemplation, the order of supreme immutability was revealed to him, that in all things he might set in order the outward action according to the inward vision. This is the case likewise with your Bride, the soul devoted to you, whoever she is. When she is brought into the Bridegroom's secret place, as a handmaid into the joy of her Lord, and thinks of you in goodness,[51] this very joy of your charity sets her wholly in order according to the pattern of your goodness

---

49. Cf. Eph 1:18.   50. Heb 8:5; cf. Ex 15:40.   51. Cf. Wis 1:1.

and conforms her thereunto. It is not that one thing is commanded here and another forbidden, but in the affection of enlightened love, nothing is permissible, nothing is pleasing if it is even slightly opposed to the harmony of order or the awareness of this joy. Blessed is she whose conscience, come weal come woe in this world, draws from heaven the pattern it should use and the manner of its life. Wherever she turns, from your countenance, O God, comes forth her judgment,[52] that she may ever be united to you by likeness in willing the same thing; for she withdraws not from you but by unlikeness in willing. Therefore whoever is a Bride has but one desire, one aspiration—namely that her face may continually be joined to your Face in the kiss of charity, that is, that she may become one spirit with you through unity of will with you;[53] that the form of her life may be ardently impressed to the form of your love, by the ardor of great love; or should the material prove unyielding, that it may be broken and set in order by the force of discipline.

But after this has been consummated, the light of your countenance, O Lord, is signed upon your Bride, your love, your beautiful one, and its gladness is set in order in her devout soul,[54] where now all duly proceeds according to the order of charity. Sleeping and taking her rest in the selfsame peace,[55] she rejoices in the Bridegroom's embrace and says: "His left hand is under my head, and his right hand shall embrace me."

52. Cf. Ps 16:2.   53. Cf. 1 Cor 6:17.
54. Cf. Ps 4:7.   55. Cf. Ps 4:9.

STANZA 11

His left hand is under my head,
And his right hand shall embrace me.[1]

THIS EMBRACE extends to man, but it surpasses man. For this embrace is the Holy Spirit. He is the Communion, the Charity, the Friendship, the Embrace of the Father and of the Son of God; and he himself is all these things in the love of Bridegroom and Bride. But on the one hand stands the majesty of consubstantial Nature; on the other, the gift of grace. On the one hand, dignity; on the other, condescension. Nevertheless it is the same, absolutely the same Spirit. True, this embrace is begun here, to be perfected elsewhere. This deep calls on another deep;[2] this ecstasy dreams of something far other than what it sees; this secret sighs for another secret; this joy evokes another joy; this sweetness foretells another sweetness. And the essence of this good and of that good is the same, but its aspect is different; the nature is the same, but the dignity is different; the sense is similar, but the majesty is different. For this belongs to mortal life and that to eternity; this to wayfaring, and that to journey's end; this to holy progress, that to consummate perfection and perfect beatitude. For when Face shall be fully revealed to face, and mutual knowledge shall be perfect, and the Bride shall know even as she is known,[3] it will then be the full kiss and the full embrace; for she will not need the left hand to

1. Song 2:6.   2. Cf. Ps 41:8.   3. Cf. 1 Cor 13:12.

106

stay her up, but the delights of the Bridegroom's right hand shall completely embrace the Bride even to the end of infinite eternity. Then, I say, it will be the full kiss and the full embrace, the power of which is the wisdom of God; its sweetness, the Holy Spirit; and its perfection, the full fruition of the Divinity, and God all in all.[4] Then faith will not flicker, and hope will not fear, because full charity in the full vision of God will exalt all affections, uniting them in effective joy and fruition. All that belonged to corruption or morality will be either dead or raised up again unto eternal life. But, in the meantime, she says: "His left hand is under my head, and his right hand shall embrace me."

133. The work of setting charity in order brings after it the relief and consolation of the sweetness the Bride needs and desires. All the torments of that work, which are sweet but nonetheless torments, are transformed by this relief and consolation into certain experiences and first fruits of a new grace, and a foretaste of future beatitude. That the Bride may already begin to sleep and rest in peace in the selfsame,[5] she is finally welcomed—not once, but as often as grace, in its work of order, will have it so—to Jesus's bosom, upon his breast, like the beloved Disciple;[6] and she is admitted to the secret places of the Son, where are hidden all the treasures of the wisdom and knowledge of God.[7] There, resting sweetly, the Bride's blessed soul is supported by the left hand of the Bridegroom. And his right hand wholly embraces her, while godliness with contentment is set in order in her.[8]

Thus the grace of spiritual consolation wholly possesses her, and the Bridegroom's tenderness does not permit her head, being the chief seat of the soul, to cleave to the earth because of any lack of bodily goods. For if now and then she has need of some, she is not allowed to feel the lack of any. A person who has possessions is certainly enslaved to them if he feels the lack of what he does not

4. Cf. Eph 1:23.   5. Cf. Ps 4:9.   6. Cf. Jn 21:20.
7. Cf. Col 2:3.   8. Cf. 1 Tim 6:6.

possess. This is why the Apostle says: "Needing nothing yet enriching many."[9] A person who desires things, feels the need of them. But he who neither desires nor loves them, whether he possesses them or possesses them not, says confidently with the Apostle: "For I have learned to be self-sufficing in whatever circumstances I am. I know how to live humbly, and I know how to live in abundance (I have been schooled in every place and every condition), to be filled and to be hungry, to have abundance and to suffer want."[10]

So far concerning the left hand which, as the Psalm says, the Lord in his nearness puts under the Bride's head that for the time being it may not be bruised.[11]

134. Speaking of the right hand and its embrace, the Apostle adds immediately: "I can do all things in him who strengthens me."[12] The embrace of the right hand, that is, of spiritual grace, strengthens the soul, that it may neither feel the lack of exterior things and those it possesses not, nor be enslaved to its possessions. As he who needs things is enslaved by them, so he who knows how to use them conquers them. For if he possesses them not, he cares not; but if he possesses them, he does not hoard them out of enslavement to them, but distributes them with liberality.

135. The Bride has the Bridegroom's left hand under her head when her soul, dedicated to God, is granted a sufficiency of temporal consolations, together with contempt for the things she does not possess. And the right hand embraces her, when spiritual consolations (for these are the right hand) both encourage her in the present and strengthen her for the future by the certitude of the eternal promises. She is pressed to the Bridegroom's heart by both the left hand and the right hand when the good use of what is temporal, the loving fruition of what is eternal, and all other things work together for her unto the love of God;[13] and she sleeps among the midst of

9. Cf. 2 Cor 6:10. 10. Phil 4:11f. 11. Cf. Ps 36:24.
12. Phil 4:13. 13. Cf. Rom 8:28.

these lots[14] when, the Bridegroom tarrying, she conducts herself patiently.[15]

136. In yet another way, well-ordered charity has a left hand and a right hand. For this embrace is indeed the embrace of charity. Charity has a right hand given to labor and a left hand inclined to repose—in other words, the exercise of the active life, busy about much serving; and zeal for contemplation, offering easy support to the Bride's head. And thus we repeat, with two arms, as it were, or two hands, the beloved Bride is drawn close to the Bridegroom's heart; that is, with the arms or hands of good works and holy contemplation, of reason and love, or of rational knowledge and efficacious wisdom.

The left hand, being less taken up with activity, is a good figure of contemplative love or wisdom, which is satisfied with the one thing it finds needful.[16] Hence it is said of wisdom, in the book by that name: "They who are less in action shall receive wisdom."[17] The right hand, likewise, is a good figure of the keen perception of reason or natural knowledge, whereof again we read: "Times shall pass over, and knowledge shall be manifold."[18] Reason, therefore, attracts the Bride, and love embraces her, while what is reasonably chosen is loved. But the Bride's head, which is the chief seat of the heart, is supported by the left hand when through the understanding of love itself, the mind, being well and lovingly disposed, enjoys what it loves. Thus both work together for their reciprocal good, while love strengthens the attraction of reason, and reason strengthens the embrace of love; love is fortified by reason, but reason is enlightened by love. Nay rather, by the preventing grace of him who predestines and chooses and calls, reason brings about love, but love affects reason until the mind, having become spiritual, judges all things and itself is judged by no man.[19]

14. Cf. Ps 67:14.
16. Cf. Lk 10:42.
18. Dan 12:4.

15. Cf. Mt 25:5.
17. Sir 38:25.
19. Cf. 1 Cor 2:15.

The right hand labors against tribulations, distress, persecutions, hunger, nakedness, danger and swords and is exercised "in labor and hardships and many sleepless nights."[20] But the left hand is patient, is kind; is not self-seeking; is not provoked, thinks no evil; does not rejoice over wickedness, but rejoices with the truth; bears with all things, believes all things, endures all things.[21] The works of the right hand are not accomplished without much labor and severe fatigue of soul and body alike; those of the left hand can be performed in repose and silence, not requiring great bodily exertion. But as we have repeatedly said already, both right hand and left hand instruct the Bride in love for the Bridegroom; and since her soul is lovingly inclined, the right hand causes and protects within it peace and lasting tranquillity, while the left hand enjoys these blessings.

137. In one of these ways or by both at once, the Bride, sleeping in the Bridegroom's embrace, is hidden sometimes in the secret of his face from the disturbance of men; she is protected in his tabernacle from the contradiction of tongues.[22] Now transported in mind to God, and now become sober for her neighbor's sake, she is always ready either to remain hidden or to show herself, according to the will of the Bridegroom who hides her and protects her. Listen, in fine, to the words of him who keeps her hidden and protected: "I have entreated you, ye daughters of Jerusalem!"

---

20. Cf. Rom 8:35; 2 Cor 6:5; 11:27.
21. Cf. 1 Cor 13:4ff.   22. Cf. Ps 30:21.

FINALE

I have entreated you,
  ye daughters of Jerusalem,
By the roes and the young harts,
That you stir not up,
  nor make the beloved to awake,
Till she please.

The voice of my Beloved![1]

T HIS ENTREATY is in reality a stringent command, that
is, an efficacious working of God's power. It is addressed to
the daughters of Jerusalem, souls who are newer and weaker
in religious life. They are entreated (each of them by the virtues she
has received) when they are inspired with fear lest, in failing to
show reverence for the secret of the nuptial chamber or neglecting
to offer loving felicitations, they should lose the grace needed to
practice virtue. They are entreated by the roes, reputed to be of
sharper sight and fond of the mountains, and by the young harts,
foes of snakes and fleet-footed, when they fear to lose the gaze of
purer contemplation, the love of heavenly things and hatred of
vices, together with the rapid and welcome success that seems to
attend their progress in virtue; they are entreated lest without
sufficient need or by excessive importunity they should presume to

1. Song 2:7f.

dishonor or disturb the joy of Bridegroom and Bride in their mutual union and fruition.

139. The Bridegroom says: "That you stir not up, nor make the beloved to awake, till she please." The Bride is forced to awake when she is disturbed in the slumber of contemplation; she is stirred up when she is called to labor. Sometimes she is pleased to awake from the quiet of her slumber, and sometimes she is not pleased, because in the slumber of contemplation it is given her to taste solely the charity of truth. This is why she has no wish to be stirred up and called away except when the truth of charity itself calls her away from the contemplation of the loved truth; and then she never refuses the needful work or service.

140. Then in her transport and ecstasy, in the slumber of quiet, the Bride hears the voice of him who entreats her; she feels the grace with which he inspires her and sees the power with which he works. She sees also that the young maidens respect her slumber without retarding their own progress. Then she says: "The voice of my Beloved!" This entreaty, this inspiration, this grace, is the voice of my Beloved; since he loves to this extent, he must be supremely loved. This peace, this sweetness, this slumber of quiet, is from the Lord; it is the voice of the Lord, preparing the young harts in order to hasten the progress of the daughters of Jerusalem. And to me, his beloved, in ecstasy of soul, he discovers the thick woods of his mysteries and his sacraments.

141. "The voice of my Beloved!" A few words, but a wealth of grace! In this state of mind, words are of no avail, but the power of spiritual understanding and devout affections reduce them to one word—the Word who is with God,[2] God the Word who is coming to be in the Bride because he is working in her. Nevertheless "voice" is better here than "word," for there is no distinction of syllables or formation by the tongue; it comes to be in the enlightened intellect by pure affection, while all the bodily senses

2. Cf. Jn 1:1.

and mental faculties are at rest and idle; this whole work is performed by the Holy Spirit's operation in the sense of love.

The voice that pronounces the word is the efficacious power of the Divinity which breaks the cedars of Libanus,[3] the arrogant ways of human wisdom and worldly pride. This voice is not heard except in the secrecy of silence; it takes effect only in a pure heart. But where it is heard, where it takes effect, it takes effect not otherwise than according to its own nature. Our word, when the speaker utters it, created as it is in letters, divided into syllables and arranged to form a word, causes something similar and in like manner in the hearer, the same letters, the same syllables, the same word. In the same way the Word of God "in the form of God,"[4] born inseparably of God, comes to be in the Bride in what he does in the Bride; and he comes to be not in an unlike manner. For whatever God the Father does, this the Son also does in like manner. And therefore when he speaks to the Bride or in the Bride, he speaks or works not anything else and not otherwise than according to his own nature and his own manner of being; not speaking or working that he might be, but of himself working in her, so that she may be in him. And when he speaks to her, he speaks himself to her; and thus it is in himself that whatever he wills her to know, he makes known to her to whom he speaks, having become wisdom for her. And whatever he wills, he brings to pass in her or through her, being himself her strength, her justifying justice and her sanctifying sanctification. And to her who is a Bride the Word of God utters himself and his Father, in the Spirit of his mouth, to such an extent that her whole consciousness is penetrated by the fullness of illuminating grace and she can barely breathe forth the flame of her heart in these few words when she says: "The voice of my Beloved!"

142. And this same voice becomes both the voice of the Bridegroom to the Bride and the voice of the Bride to the Bridegroom, in the joy of the mutual union and fruition in which they constantly

3. Cf. Ps 28:5.   4. Cf. Phil 2:6.

L

converse and answer one another. It is the goodness of him who gives and the love of her who receives. Thus in the cellar of wine, in the fervor and joy of consummated charity, upon the bed of conscience in full flower, takes place in union that blessed repose of Bridegroom and Bride which that very Bridegroom promised saying: "If anyone love me, he shall be loved of my Father: and I will love him and will manifest myself to him: and we will come to him and make our abode with him."[5]

143. O Love of loves, to whom homage is paid by this Song of Songs, which a loveless person can recite after a fashion, but no one can sing except a lover and a true lover! You know what my heart's ambitions are in studying your canticle, O Spirit, you who search all things[6] and have knowledge of every voice![7] Far be it from the heart and intention of your poor servant to seek and envisage in this study any purpose but one—that by seeing your splendor and experiencing your charity, my conscience may be enlightened in you and my soul purified by your influence; and that by pondering these songs which pertain to you and impart your delightful taste and sweet perfume, I may savor your taste and perceive your fragrance, and my life may be wholly molded in you and by your influence.

144. Come in the abundance of your blessings, come to me your servant, into my heart, your own place—that place for the Lord, that tabernacle for the God of Jacob[8] which I cannot find for you unless you first find it for me. And until I find it for you, I will not go up into the bed wherein I lie, I will never give sleep to my eyes or slumber to my eyelids.[9] Thanks be to you, through the first fruits of your Spirit my detestable loves of olden time, which being alien to you alienated me from you, are now no longer. Your knowledge bears witness in my conscience that I love you alone,

5. Jn 14:23.   6. Cf. 1 Cor 2:10.   7. Cf. Wis 1:7.
8. Cf. Ps 131:5.   9. Cf. Ps 131:3f.

with a unique love, always assuredly by a free judgment of reason; and, when my spirit is able to be free and master of itself, with the entire love of my soul. But a few remnants of my loves of olden time yet fill my memory, like bodiless shades or forms lacking substance; and without the consent of my will, a few impressions of vain and empty delight invade my thoughts. Thus my conscience is tainted and can hardly deserve even now and then to love you in all purity. Until you fully transform my captivity to these things, I can never fully aspire to your liberty, your purity, your stability. But one day with the wealth of your plenitude and the delights of your goodness, you will come within your poor servant and begin to show him, by indubitable experience and awareness, how truly you, O God, are charity; and how there is identity between God and his love; joy in the Holy Spirit and the Holy Spirit; the sweetness of loving and the beginning of fruition; love itself and the understanding thereof. At that moment, while Charity prays and pleads for us and in our favor with unutterable groanings[10] and omniscient love, and reason passes beyond desire and contemplates you, O love, with fruition, the sacrifice of praise offered by your child through your canticle shall glorify you, and this shall be the way by which you will show him the salvation of God.[11]

In the meantime let my poor and miserable love, struggling and groping, follow as it is led and yearn as it is called, through these metaphors of divine love and its own imperfection, toward your perfection. As long as it walks by faith and not by sight, may it use devoutly and wisely these rudiments it has acquired, until this outward dramatic allegory becomes in it a true story. Then all will be able to see, in your light, how much the devotion of the simplest lover surpasses, in your judgment, the prudence of the most learned thinker; for where reason draws back, devout love itself will become its own understanding.

10. Cf. Rom 8:26.　　　　11. Cf. Ps 49:23.

SECOND SONG

PRELUDE OR ARGUMENT

THUS FAR we have set forth in one way or another the first "repose" in the joy of the nuptial feast. We have matched it, to the best of our power, with the Song belonging to it, which seems to be devoted to the first steps of novice fervor. With God's help let us go on to the second Song, in the course of which the Bride renews herself, by more prudent patience and more experienced prudence, for the Bridegroom's second embrace.

146. In the first place, however, we must briefly examine the historical sense of the Song which is to follow, setting the spiritual sense parallel to it.[1] As we learn from the Books of Paralipomenon, King Solomon, the king of peace, enjoyed peace in his kingdom, since his nearby enemies had been subdued. After building in Jerusalem the Lord's house and the royal house, he declared: "My wife shall not dwell in the house of my father David, King of Israel, for it is sanctified, because the ark of the Lord came into it."[2] Consequently he erected a house outside Jerusalem on Libanus[3] for his Egyptian wife, the daughter of Pharaoh, and commanded her to live far from the royal house until she should have laid aside completely her barbarous nature, and all her Egyptian mannerisms. The king went out to visit her from time to time, and from time to time she was called into the city and entered the royal house and

1. This was also St Bernard's usual order in commenting on the Song of Songs; see e.g. Sermons 42, 46, 51, 56, 58, 59, etc.
2. Cf. 2 Chron 8:11.   3. Cf. 1 Kings 7:2.

the king's chamber, not to dwell there but as it were to catch a glimpse of the king's glory and enjoy for a short space the favor of the royal chamber, returning afterwards to her own abode.

In the same manner Christ, the King of eternal peace, the Bridegroom of the Church brought together from among the nations, the Bridegroom of the faithful soul snatched from the darkness of sin (for "Egypt" means darkness), after the resurrection of his flesh, death being swallowed up in victory,[4] received his kingdom in the heavenly Jerusalem. He then commanded his Bride—separated, as long as she lives in the flesh, because of her mortal condition, from the glory of dwelling together with him above the heavens—to rest in the abode prepared for her. This command he gave at the moment of his ascension into heaven, when he said to his disciples: "Wait here in the city, until you are endued with power from on high."[5] He said this to his disciples then by reason of the promised coming of the Holy Spirit; and he says it to all the sons of the Bridegroom down to this very day by reason of his promise to dwell with them always until the end of the world, and the intermittent favor of his more palpable and more manifest visitations. This city is the Church, built, for the time of the pilgrimage of this life, on Libanus, that is, on the lovely mountain of grace that imparts whiteness. For "Libanus" means whiteness. There dwells the Egyptian princess, the Bride of Christ, the faithful soul, to whom God's grace, in the faith of the Church, is to impart whiteness until she is wholly pure. With anxious devotion the Bride constantly directs her heart to the place where she has already laid up her treasure;[6] every day she expects and receives the daily visitation of divine power, with which she is endowed from on high,[7] until at length she is freed from the bond of the flesh and deserves to be permitted to dwell together with her Bridegroom eternally. Here, therefore, in the Church, in the unity

4. Cf. 1 Cor 15:54.   5. Lk 24:49.
6. Cf. Mt 6:21.   7. Cf. Lk 1:78.

of faith, she who is a Bride is frequently enlightened by the grace of an interior visitation; often by the power of contemplation the Bride with devout love follows after the Bridegroom until she attains the vision of heavenly peace and is found worthy of the royal marriage chamber. But the burden of earthly life weighs her down, and she is never permitted to remain there for a long time. When she has received the pledge of the Spirit of the Bridegroom and has left with him the pledge of her own spirit, she is quickly sent back from the contemplation of the Bridegroom's riches to the house of her poverty, knowing to some extent what is wanting to her.[8]

Here we have the entire sequence of the plot of this holy love song from beginning to end, its entire matter and action. The scenes are already marked out and harmoniously arranged: hope hastens, desire becomes a crucifixion, wisdom sets all in order, love speeds forward, and grace is there to meet it; until finally, at the end of the Song, the grief of the soul's desire is turned into the joy of fruition, the weariness of delay being at last exchanged for mutual union.

8. Cf. Ps 38:5.

STANZA 1

The voice of my Beloved!

Behold, it is he! He comes
   leaping upon the mountains,
Skipping over the hills.
My beloved is like a roe and a young hart.
See! He himself stands behind our wall,
Looking through the windows,
   peering through the lattices.
See! My Beloved speaks to me![1]

WHEN the Bride comes to herself again after the first ecstasy of the first "repose," in which she was transported in mind to God, and becomes sober, returning to herself,[2] she muses on the memory of the sweetness she has tasted and longs for a place of retirement after the consummation of sacred affections. She flees the crowd and loves to sit in the concealment of her cell, in solitude of heart and retreat of conscience, that she may zealously purify her heart and eagerly cleanse her face in a glass and in riddle, so that one day she may see face to face.[3] For here she who is a Bride, as the Apostle says, cleaving to One alone, is not divided but concerned solely about the things of the Lord, how she may please the Lord,[4] whose approval she has secured. She strives to become

1. Song 2:8ff.
2. Cf. 2 Cor 5:13.
3. Cf. 1 Cor 13:12.
4. Cf. 1 Cor 7:32.

holy in body and spirit,[5] without stain of sin or deceitful pretence; she strives after what is virtuous and what affords her an opportunity to fix her attention on the Lord. Waiting in suspense for the Bridegroom's return, his voice, his face, she suddenly hears a faint murmur as if he were coming from a distance and conversing the while with companions on the way. Thereupon she exclaims: "The voice of my Beloved!"

148. These words—"the voice of my Beloved!"—may apply both to what has gone before and to what is going to follow. They may mark the end of the first "repose" and the beginning of the second. This also seems particularly appropriate to the subject in hand; for as from the evening of the day that is past springs the morning light of the morrow, so the close of a day in the interior life often proves to be the beginning and cause of another day.

149. The Bride says therefore: "The voice of my Beloved!" And leaping up to go and meet him when he comes, she exclaims: "Behold, it is he!" The Bridegroom's voice, addressing the Bride, is the sudden grace granted to her as a lover, which imparts good dispositions to her memory; his words are the affection prepared for her understanding. And so when the Bride hears the voice of the Bridegroom as he comes, she cries: "Behold!" And when she hears his words, once he is present and conversing with her, she says, as if pointing him out with her finger: "It is he!" Moreover the Bride goes to meet the Word of God when her devout affection longs eagerly for understanding. And she sees him coming when she feels within herself the working of his mercy. For what is his mercy toward us but his goodness anticipating us in all things?

But by a more intimate and more personal understanding of love, the Bride contemplates the coming of the Bridegroom to her when she experiences in her soul all the ways in which he comes to her, both in their effects and in her affections. For she contemplates how the God of the mountains comes toward the mountains, and how

5. Cf. 1 Cor 7:34.

he comes toward the hills; and what she contemplates in them, she experiences within herself, as we have said. She sees him coming to the mountains, leaping upon the mountains, and coming to the hills, skipping over the hills. A mountain is earth that is lifted up above the earth; this is an image of the chosen soul, in whom, through the love of heavenly things in contemplation, human nature is elevated above what pertains to man. The faithful soul that is stronger in this love is a mountain; the soul that is weaker is a hill. The former is a mountain ascending, by an inner experience of justice, from humility of heart to the heights of hope; the latter is a hill, being likewise established after its own manner in the same grace of hope by God's grace and an inner experience of fruitful penance. The one has risen to the heights of justice, but it is founded in humility; the other, however, even when its justice exalts it in God's sight, of its own accord holds itself in check and sinks itself within itself, through the fear born of a humble conscience. As for the leaps of the Bridegroom, it is to them the prophet refers when he says: "He has rejoiced as a giant to run the way. His going out is from the end of heaven, and his circuit even to the end thereof."[6]

150. When, therefore, the Bride contemplates the Bridegroom's going out from the end of heaven and his circuit even to the end thereof, and between these two poles sees him coming from heaven into the womb, from the womb into the manger, from the manger to the cross, from the cross into the sepulchre and from the sepulchre into heaven—does she not wonder at his marvellous leaps, as it were, over the heights of such great works, which are comparable to lofty mountain peaks? And when, by the breath of his love, the Bridegroom pours into the understanding of certain great men faith in these leaps, what is he doing save leaping upon the mountains? But leaping upon the mountains, he skips over the hills; for this understanding passes over the heads of many who are in the body of the faithful. As the Bridegroom comes to the Bride,

6. Ps 18:6.

therefore, he leaps upon the mountains and skips over the hills, when he raises some souls to the heights by the grace of contemplation and assigns to others a place in the lower regions of necessary activity.

These are the leaps and bounds by which men of earth raise themselves to heaven, when from the consideration of God's works and his great bounty to us, the charity of God is poured forth in our hearts by the Holy Spirit who is given to us.[7] By the love of the Spirit, the leaps of human efforts do, indeed, soar from the depths to the heights; but it is from above, from the Father of lights, that they receive the force to attain their effect.[8] This is why, when holy exultation is felt by souls who leap, the impulses are a sort of dance of the mind which surpasses man's experience and manner of acting; its liveliness and loftiness are greater, in proportion to the sweetness of the experiences which draw the soul to leap. But these leaps are those of the mountains the Bridegroom leaps upon, not of the hills he skips over; the hills stand rooted and grounded in faith,[9] yet they do not feel the tread of him who skips over them, that is, they do not feel the action of grace.

But as one who leaps from the earth very quickly falls back, so the coming of the Bridegroom to the Bride is still a long time away. Nevertheless, as soon as he draws nearer, he will transform those leaps into the approaches of light of which it is said: "Approach him and be enlightened,"[10] those ascending steps of which the same prophet says: "Blessed is the man whose help is from you. In his heart he has disposed to ascend by steps, in the vale of tears, in the place which he has established. For the Lawgiver shall give a blessing; they shall go from virtue to virtue; the God of gods shall be seen in Sion."[11] But in the meantime the Bridegroom comes, as we have said, leaping and skipping.

7. Cf. Rom 5:5.   8. Cf. Jas 1:17.   9. Cf. Eph 3:17.
10. Ps 33:6.   11. Ps 83:6ff.

151. Or if you will, these leaps and bounds may be understood otherwise.[12] For instance, in the mountains, that is, in the saints, the Bridegroom's leaps are unhampered by the obstacle of sin; but in the hills, that is, in the less perfect, his bounds are not free from hindrances; nevertheless, he leaps without stumbling; he skips over all things, forgiving sins and imparting grace. The just and perfect man also leaps upon the way leading to God; that is, he advances freely. He who is as yet less perfect, finds something to stumble over; but all the same he skips valiantly over every contradiction, whether it comes from himself or from someone else.

152. Next follows: "My Beloved is like a roe and a young hart." The Bridegroom, in his coming, is now drawing nearer to the Bride; even if not yet face to face, he already introduces himself to her under figures more nearly resembling the reality. And he shows himself to her sometimes through certain affections which participate in the divine power and goodness, and at other times through the effects of the divine dispensation concerning his humanity.

The word "God" [*Deus*], that name particularly appropriate, so to speak, for his divine nature, comes from the Greek, as no one doubts. It is derived either from the word θεωρῶ or the word θέω; or better, from both these words, since θεωρῶ means "I see," and θέω, "I run."[13] For what runs more swiftly than that stable motion

12. It is rather unusual for William to offer alternate interpretations of the spiritual sense of Scripture texts for his reader to choose from; however, it is quite common in St Bernard; see e.g. Sermons 22, 26, 28, 29, 30, 45, 51, 54, 60, 71 of the *Sermons on the Song of Songs*. In Sermon 51 he says explicitly: "Surely no person of prudence will find fault with me for giving various interpretations of the same text, provided nothing is said anywhere contrary to truth. For charity, which every part of Scripture is intended to subserve, will be able to accomplish its work of edification the more efficaciously, in proportion to the number of apt expositions discoverable for each passage . . . There should be no objection to the practice of drawing out from any single text of Scripture a variety of apt significations, suited to the necessity or the use of different souls."—no. 4.

13. This same etymology for the word *Deus* is found in St Gregory of Nyssa's commentary on the Song of Songs, PG 44:862.

which, remaining stable in itself, moves all things? What travels so swiftly through the universe as he who spoke and all things were made?[14] Moreover he in whom all things are, easily sees all things at the same time and sees all beings in himself.

153. The Divine Nature in the Bridegroom is denoted by the roe because the roe is swift of pace and keen of sight. And by the young harts the human nature in the Bridegroom is quite happily expressed. Certainly Christ the man appeared in the world like a young hart, that is, as a son of the Jews. He is "the beloved son of unicorns;"[15] he is also the son of the harts, which are "multicorns"—for the hart seems to have many horns branching out from one horn. The Jews are "unicorns," that is, they trust solely in the justice of the Law; they are also "multicorns," glorying in the commandments, ceremonies and multiple observances of the Law. Christ, then, the son of the Jews, appeared in this world as a young hart; he was the new man who without sin came into the world and without sin lived in the world. As Scripture says: "most agreeable hind and most agreeable fawn,"[16] he appeared as the most agreeable Son of the most agreeable Virgin, anointed with the oil of gladness above his fellows.[17]

He comes daily to his Bride, the faithful soul, like the roe of keen sight and swift course, when he purifies and renders effective in her the eye of contemplation and brings to swift success the service she renders by her good deeds. For by a wonderful condescension of grace, the Wisdom of God, when he comes into the soul, subjugates man's intellect and conforms it to himself; and thus through illuminating grace and the enlightened understanding, there ensues in an ineffable manner a sort of composite wisdom embracing all virtues. Thus the man of God is borne toward God, and nevertheless his soul, in the outward and humbler aspects of his sanctity, does not renounce the fulfillment of the virtues. In contemplation

14. Cf. Ps 32:9.   15. Cf. Ps 28:6.
16. Cf. Prov 5:19.   17. Cf. Ps 44:8.

he sees, and in action he runs. Uniformity could never be achieved in a single man out of such diverse elements unless it came about through a certain loving and efficacious conformity between the Word of God and human intelligence, the grace of God and human devotion.

He comes to her also as the young hart, that is as the Son of man, in the following way. Long ago when he came into the world he brought to his Bride, the Church, the sacrament of the humanity he had assumed, as a pledge of love. And now in like manner he inspires in the faithful soul with greater effectiveness the faithful memory of this same grace as an incentive to charity.

Thus the Bridegroom, in his relation to the Bride, resembles a roe or a young hart, when by means of certain "manifestations" or "theophanies," he feeds her in her hunger and comforts her in her affliction; and nothing but his countenance fills her with joy.[18] As he comes, moreover, he does not continually leap and skip; sometimes he approaches her and stands still. With a certain added joy he gives himself to her, and with more abundant grace he consoles the irksomeness of her desires, the weariness of her efforts and the devotion of her love. And so she exclaims: "Behold, he stands behind our wall!"

154. Here it should be noted that when the Bride saw him coming she said: "Behold, it is he!"[19] And now that she sees him approaching her she says: "Behold, it is he himself." In other words, this is he in person, for he is he who is; he no longer shows himself to me in a prophet, an angel or an apostle; but beyond the glass and the riddle, he shows himself, to a certain extent, in himself. He whom she affirms is he himself has drawn near to her, as she acknowledges, not merely by the sense of grace but also by the sweetness of experience; to such a degree that in that hour, or in that time of the divine visitation, only the wall of this mortal life holds back Bridegroom and Bride from the full kiss of mutual

18. Cf. Ps 16:11.   19. Song 2:8.

union and the full embrace of mutual fruition. And this is he himself to whom Moses said: "Show me yourself";[20] and the Lord replied to Moses: "Man shall not see me and live."[21] To see the Invisible behind the wall, means therefore to see him insofar as is possible in this life.

155. "See!" she says, "he himself stands behind our wall." "See!" expresses the sense of presence; "he himself," the joy of experience; "stands," the sweetness of fruition. Or it is that wall of separation between Bridegroom and Bride, of which the prophet says: "Through my God I shall go over a wall."[22] What is this wall if not a mind, memory and conscience corrupted by outward things (through the concupiscence of the flesh and the eyes, and the ambition of life) and incapable, while in this state, of affection for God? This explains what the prophet says of persons of this kind: "How long does he load himself with thick clay?"[23] And elsewhere: "Your sins set up a barrier between you and God."[24]

But since through this thick wall of clay no way of contemplation opens to allow the Bride to see the Bridegroom, you, O Desire of her soul, make yourself nevertheless direct windows in it through which you may look at her directly, and oblique lattices through which you may peer at her as it were covertly. The direct windows are your justices which are right, rejoicing upright hearts;[25] the oblique lattices are the devices of your goodness and mercy, coming as it were covertly when they are neither deserved nor hoped for. Through the windows, you look with approval at the Bride's good deeds; through the lattices, you peer with pity at whatever in her has need of your mercy. Thus by first looking at her, you enable her to see you; by standing before her, you make her stable toward you; until he who pities and she who loves mutually draw near, and

20. Cf. Ex 33:13, 18.   21. Ex 33:20.
22. Ps 17:30.   23. Heb 2:6.
24. Cf. Is 59:2; William is quoting freely here.
25. Cf. Ps 18:9.

this encounter completely breaks down the enmity of sin, the intervening wall of separation.[26] Then come mutual vision, mutual embrace, mutual joy and unity of spirit.

In the meantime, the Bride sometimes goes over the wall not by herself but in you, O Lord her God; and she is admitted to clearer understanding, more perfect knowledge and sweeter love. Not only does she experience the fountain of life which is with you and the light in your light,[27] but she is also allowed for a while to stand still and enjoy fruition with such deep feeling, such strong affection and such clear understanding that, as we have already said, it seems to her as if only the interstice of human mortality separates her from the perfection of full vision. This is what she means when she says: "See! He himself stands behind our wall."

156. This, she says, is he himself, he to whom Moses said: "Show me yourself."[28] And the Psalmist said: "But you are always the selfsame."[29] When he first appeared to her, she did not yet see him as himself; she merely saw him leaping over the mountains and skipping over the hills; but now it is he himself, standing still. There is a great difference between "he" and "himself." "He" is someone pointed to outwardly, with one's finger, so to speak; but "he himself" glories in the Bride herself and delights in her. "He" appears in the motion of leaps and bounds; "he himself" in the stability of the good soul. The interjection *En*—"See!"—indicates closer proximity than *Ecce*—"Behold!" *Ecce* shows something that is perceptible to the senses, even though far away; but *En* points out something within hand's reach, or in the hand.

157. "Behind our wall." My wall, says the Bride, had been that of mortality, by the condition of sin common to the human race, and the corruption and affliction of nature. But the Bridegroom, when he drew near me, made it his, by the condescension of his grace and the compassion of his goodness. Therefore she calls it "our wall,"

---

26. Cf. Eph 2:14.   27. Cf. Ps 35:10.
28. Cf. Ex 33:13.   29. Ps 101:28.

in which mercy and truth met each other,[30] when after the sin of the first man, the truth and the severity of the truth built up for me this wall of common mortality; and in the time to have mercy, mercy built up the same wall for itself.

In it, as we have already said, there are windows and lattices; the direct windows of the Lord who is just and loves justice;[31] and the oblique lattices of him who forgives much to the sinner that loves much.[32] As the Bridegroom draws near the Bride, he looks through the windows and peers through the lattices. When he is nigh to her that calls upon him in truth,[33] he attracts her to himself, both by the things pertaining to his divinity and by the things pertaining to his humanity; showing them to her after his own manner, that she may contemplate each of them in himself, he feeds the affection of his lover solemnly with both.

158. But for the soul seeking God there is likewise a window by which it may contemplate God—the eye of reason; through reason, with the help of illuminating grace, it explores spiritual and divine things. This eye was created in man chiefly that God might be seen by him through it. By the illuminating light of the sun, the eye of the body, where its gaze is not cut off by any obstacle or by obscurity in the air, can go on seeing wherever it turns, until sight fails in it because of its natural weakness. In the same way, by the action of illuminating grace, reason, when it tends in the direction of divine contemplation, unless it lets itself be affected from without by the darkness of error, suffers no contradiction in regarding the simplicity and purity of the divine substance, until, overwhelmed by glory, it grows weary and falls back on itself.

159. There are yet other windows through which the Bride regards the Bridegroom: piety, charity and wisdom. They are

30. Cf. Ps 84:11.
32. Cf. Lk 7:47.

31. Cf. Ps 10:8.
33. Cf. Ps 144:18.

M

called "the worship of God."[34] When through these windows she gazes in contemplation on the joy of the Bridegroom and comprehends something spiritual or divine, the Bridegroom sees her, or rather enables her to see.

But as for the dispensation of the Mediator in time, the lattice through which the Bride directs her contemplation is the faith in temporal things whereby she is raised up to eternal realities. In this faith the gaze of the contemplator of God is obliged to turn in an oblique direction; for in the one Person of Christ it marvels, without the shadow of doubt, at the mystery of two natures, and adores the one and the other in the Mediator, in the unity of his Person. When human reason, through this lattice, considers the humiliation he assumed, it seems to its own eyes to be turning not a little in an oblique direction in its flight toward God, until grace illumines faith so that God who is man, and the Man who is God, begins to be not only believed in but understood. Then the contemplative soul begins to be fed, with supreme delight, by one and the same light, from both the window and the lattice. Now that the soul understands, the Spirit speaks of mysteries; the Word of God speaks of himself, and his word runs swiftly to its fulfillment,[35] since in him to whom it is spoken, the things heard with understanding come to pass efficaciously. For he arises and makes haste and does whatever the sentence that follows seems to command or teach. And this is what follows: "See! My Beloved speaks to me: 'Arise, make haste, my love, my dove, my beautiful one, and come'!"[36]

---

34. William here quotes from the Septuagint version (or some Latin translation taken from it, rather than the Vulgate): Job 28:28. He cites the same verse in the *Letter to the Carthusians of Mont Dieu,* no. 66, trans. Shewring, p. 114.

35. Cf. Ps 147:15.   36. Song 2:10.

STANZA 2

Arise, make haste, my love, my dove,
    my beautiful one, and come!
For winter is now past,
    the rain is over and gone.

The flowers have appeared in our land;
    the time of pruning is come.
The voice of the turtledove
    is heard in our land.

The fig tree has put forth her green figs;
    the vines in flower have yielded their sweet smell.[1]

HE CALLS her "love" or "friend" when he makes her his friend by making known to her all things that he has heard from his Father.[2] He calls her "dove" when he makes her his own, that is, capable of receiving the Holy Spirit as he appeared upon the Lord at his baptism;[3] he exhorts her to take to herself the wings of spiritual understanding and fly away to the solitude of the heart[4] and the secrecy of a guileless conscience. He calls her "beautiful," for once again he has conformed her to his image and likeness, according to man's original state.[5] He commands her not only to arise and come but also to make haste; that is, not merely to love

1. Song 2:10ff.   2. Cf. Jn 15:15.   3. Cf. Mt 3:16.
4. Cf. Ps 54:7f.   5. Cf. Gen 1:26f.; Wis 2:23.

but to love passionately. He commands her to rise above earthly things, when he inspires her with disgust for all earthly things. He commands her to come, and he draws her; he commands her to make haste, and he constrains her.

In this way, therefore, the Bride says, my Beloved speaks to me. That is, the Word of God is accomplished in the heart of her who hears and loves, when, as we have said, to hear the omnipotent Word of God includes the fulfillment of what has been heard. It is heard sometimes by the bodily senses, for instance by sight in reading and by hearing in instruction; and sometimes by the grace of inner inspiration, calling her who hears from the flesh to the spirit and from the senses to interior understanding, that she may live not in the flesh but in the spirit. The Bridegroom brings this to pass when he says, "Arise!" He banishes sluggishness when he says, "Make haste!" He attracts love when he says, "My love!" He confers grace when he says, "My dove!" And he brings her life and virtues into harmony when he says, "My beautiful one!"

161. Then he adds: "The winter is now past, the rain is over and gone," when—God disposing us for it—he causes the winter of personal disorders to pass and puts to flight the storms of vices. First he urges her to arise, and she obeys. Then lest she faint from fear of temptations, he tells her that the winter and rains are over, now that the whirlwind of vices has been calmed, and the pleasant season of the holy virtues presents itself as if of its own accord. Hitherto, hidden and cowering amid the winter of temptations and the storms of vices, she was content to remain in safety, keeping herself to herself; she had neither care nor anxiety save for herself; no happiness outside herself; no flowers from the divine Scriptures; never the grace of spiritual joys nor the fruits of the Spirit, which are signified by the fragrance and flowers of the vine and the green figs of the fig tree; no retreat in the deeper things of the more secret wisdom, signified by the turtledove, which in remote localities, away from crowds, speaks mysteries among the perfect. But now she hears this invitation:

162. "Arise, make haste, my love, my dove, my beautiful one, and come! For winter is now past, the rain is over and gone. The flowers have appeared in our land; the time of pruning is come; the voice of the turtledove is heard in our land; the fig tree has put forth her green figs; the vines in flower have yielded their sweet smell."

163. After this, the same names implying familiarity and favor are repeated again, and the Bride is once more commanded to arise, make haste and come. She is awakened first by prevenient grace and then by a judgment elicited thereupon by her own reason and free will; and while her conscience bears her witness that we are the sons of God,[6] the goodness of him who awakens her commends itself to her more sweetly and familiarly. This is the sense of the verses that come next.

6. Cf. Rom 9:1; 8:16.

STANZA 3

Arise, make haste, my love, my Bride,
   and come!
My dove in the clefts of the rock,
In the hollow places of the wall,
Show me your face!
Let your voice sound in my ears,
For your voice is sweet,
   and your face comely![1]

"ARISE, make haste, my love, my Bride, and come! My dove in the clefts of the rock, in the hollow places of the wall!" And these words come to pass: the Bride does what the Bridegroom urges her to do. Winter is gone and calm weather ensues; the Bridegroom appears, and the Bride is carried away with joy. She sets out willingly; the Bridegroom promises yet greater happiness, and she willingly follows his footsteps wherever he goes,[2] out of the house, out of the city, that is, beyond the natural limits of human condition, beyond the habits of an ordinary way of life; in the mysteries of the Son, which are the clefts of the rock; in the secrets of the law, which are the hollow places of the wall. For the rock which is Christ is not closed in on all sides, but has clefts through which God is revealed; and the wall of the law, by which

---

1. Song 2:13f.   2. Cf. Rev 14:4.

two peoples are separated,[3] has in the Word of God, which is more piercing than any two-edged sword,[4] passages through which differences and oppositions are reconciled. There also it is the time of pruning; because when plants first come up, many that are useless and harmful are sure to come up among the useful ones, unless they are very carefully cut away.

165. The text continues: "Show me your face; let your voice sound in my ears! For your voice is sweet, and your face comely!" The dove usually nests in the clefts of the rock and the hollow places of the wall. From there she shows her face and makes her voice heard; her face is pleasing, her voice plaintive. What does this symbolize if not the soul which, established in Christ and in faith in him, brings forth the fruits of the Spirit, lifts up to God a welcome voice of praise and, in her hope of things to come, laments their deferment? The Bride shows this face to the Bridegroom, according to his desire, when in the light of his countenance[5] her pure conscience delights to be seen by its Creator. The Bride's voice is sweet in the Bridegroom's ears when he hears it exactly as she utters it, that is, as love expresses it.

166. Let us go back a little over what we have said and review our development, according to the order of events and the sense of the words.

The Bride was sitting all by herself, awaiting the Bridegroom's return; she possessed the Spirit as the pledge that he would come back speedily; she prayed, wept and longed for him to return. And suddenly she seemed to hear something before she could discern anything with her eyes; she felt the presence of the divinity with her interior sense, although her intelligence could not grasp it. Then she exclaimed: "The voice of my Beloved!" All the senses of the faithful soul thrill with joyousness, and she springs forward

---

3. We have an illusion here to Eph 2:14ff.: Christ who makes two people to be one.

4. Cf. Heb 4:12.   5. Cf. Ps 88:16.

to meet him. She has gone but a little way when she sees him coming toward her, leaping in his haste; he skips over men of little faith, who are incapable of enduring his approach and his haste; he leaps over all understanding and skips over all reasoning.

As she sees him coming toward her, she recollects herself interiorly so that she may receive him; she feels that he is drawing near her, that he is standing behind the wall. As she sees him looking through the windows, peering through the lattices, offering himself according to her desire, she begins to understand by experience the mysteries of divine Love: that if he withdraws from her so often, it is to make her seek him more ardently; and if he sometimes surrenders himself to her who loves him, it is to prevent her from being engrossed in excessive sadness. Whenever, at the sound of his voice calling and urging her, she rises and makes haste to see and lay hold of him, suddenly he who has appeared disappears, and with him all the spiritual and divine charm of vines and flowers. He who is the source of sweetness withdraws, and all his sweetness follows him, with all his delights—the beauty of the flowers, the fragrance of the vineyards, the richness of the fruit. She who is his love loses the confidence of friendship; his dove loses her comeliness of face and sweetness of voice; his beautiful one, the grace of conformity to God. His love remains in her solitude, his dove in her lament, his beautiful one in her bereft condition. The clefts of the rock are closed, the hollow places of the wall are stopped up; they no longer offer a resting place to the dove who has no heart left.

STANZA 4

Catch us the little foxes that destroy the vines:
For our vineyard has blossomed.

My Beloved belongs to me, and I to him;
He feeds among the lilies
Till the day break,
And the shadows retire.[1]

OTHER troubles are yet in store. Little foxes force their way
into the blossoming vineyards; this means that little suggestions made by the enemy very subtly harm well-disposed
souls; or that deceitful and scandalous instigations destroy the little
vines. For the text may be understood in two ways: "Catch us the
little foxes that destroy the vines" or "Catch us the foxes that destroy
the little vines."

168. Foxes destroy the little vines; the more developed vines fear
them not. For only little ones take scandal, as the Lord points out:
"He that shall scandalize one of these little ones."[2] The Bride says:
"Catch us the foxes." Anyone who possesses the power of discerning spirits catches these foxes when he quickly detects the deceitful-
ness of sin stealing in unawares and keeps control over his appetites.
It is wisdom on the part of the Bride to ask to have the foxes caught
for her, that is, for her advantage. She asks this of the holy doctors

---

1. Song 2:15ff. 2. Mt 18:6.

or her angel guardians,[3] but never of her own sense or her own virtue, as though she trusted enough in herself to think she could catch them for herself. This is one of the ways whereby, when persons undergo temptation, it becomes clear which of them is tempted that he may be proved, and which that he may be disapproved; for the former, in his temptations, relies on no one so little as on himself; but the latter relies on no one except himself. It is for the Bride's advantage that the foxes are caught, because it is most beneficial for her salvation that her vineyard be preserved inviolate for the Bridegroom. "For," she says, "our vineyard has blossomed."

169. She whose vineyard is still in bloom—that is, whose soul is in hope—is not entirely abandoned. For the Bride is sometimes abandoned by the Bridegroom, but not for so long a time that she abandons him who has abandoned her! She humbly rejoices in his presence, and patiently endures his absence. She is the vineyard of the Lord of Hosts, of whom the Lord says to the prophet: "I bought her to me, and I said to her: 'You shall wait for me many days; you shall not play the harlot, and you shall be no man's; and I also will wait for you'."[4] This is why the Bride, who is also the vineyard, goes on to say: "My Beloved belongs to me, and I to him; he feeds among the lilies, till the day break, and the shadows retire."

170. O happy soul, O blessed conscience, true Bride of the Bridegroom! She is abandoned, and her voice takes on this accent; what in her is sin, would be holiness in souls of lesser stature; what in her is defection, would be perfection in the daughters of the Bridegroom. A man is blessed when the Lord is his God,[5] and he is wholly his; and when God's grace in him, insofar as it attracts his conscience, has already restored nature. For the state in which a good soul finds itself is not the same thing as the attraction of love;

3. St Bernard, who frequently speaks of the angels in his *Sermons on the Song of Songs* (e.g. Sermons 5, 7, 19 27, 30, 41, etc.), brings out especially their role as guardians of souls seeking God; see especially Sermons 31 and 39.

4. Hos 3:2f.   5. Cf. Ps 143:15.

and the due balance of restored nature, firmly renewed in God by the operation of grace, is not the same thing as the uplifting of this balanced nature unto God, for a moment, for an hour, by the loving attraction of the same grace. The one pertains to the Bride who is accepted; the other, to the Bride who is perfect.

171. "My Beloved," she says, "belongs to me, and I to him." Other beloveds, she says, belong to other brides; but my Beloved belongs to me. Other brides belong to other beloveds; but I belong to him alone. This is not the voice of a conscience that plays the harlot amid strange loves; it is not the profession of timorous faith and irresolute love, or of a troubled conscience or hesistant purpose. O ever happy soul, I repeat, O blessed conscience, who during her prolonged sojourning in this life,[6] while she awaits the Bridegroom's slow approach, possesses this consolation! In the heat of this world's malice, it is the feeling of hope, refeshing shade, relief of pain, lightening of labor, incentive to love and enlargement of heart in the anguish of this life; and for the future, it is the certitude of faith and expectation. Such was he who said: "In all things we suffer tribulation, but we are not distressed; we are sore pressed, but we are not destitute; we endure persecution, but we are not forsaken; we are cast down, but we do not perish," and so forth.[7]

172. This state of the good soul is piety which, according to Job, is the worship of God;[8] according to the Apostle it is profitable in all respects, since it has the promise of the present life as well as of that which is to come.[9] It is the form of faith and virtue, capable of receiving spiritual graces, fit for sacred affections, always close to God's thoughts. To the souls who are established in this state the Apostle says: "Stand fast thus in the Lord, my dearly beloved."[10] And again: "Still in what we have attained, let us also continue therein."[11]

6. Cf. Ps 119: 5.
8. Cf. Job 28:28.
10. Phil 4:1.

7. 2 Cor 4:8f.
9. Cf. 1 Tim 4:8.
11. Cf. Phil 3:16.

Up to this point, however, the flowers are still those of the blossoming vineyard; they are the hope of fruit but not real fruit. But just now, upon those who are coming up from the vale of tears, there begins to blow from the region of heavenly beatitude a breeze of truth, the sweeter fragrance of the Bridegroom's perfumes. From the mystery of divine love it brings to the advancing soul, the loving Bride, the first fruits of the Spirit in greater abundance, sweeter affection and surer experiences; the more frequent and the sweeter these last become, the more they glorify the charity of a purer life; and they themselves are the recompense of purity. The soul possesses in itself the habits of a balanced life, just as the sound body possesses its health. But all these things belong to the good soul, as health does to the sound body, either for necessary uses or for the will's desires. As the health of the body is, to a certain extent, unaware of itself and esteems itself but lightly until it is used to serve necessity or the will, so the health of the soul is unaware of itself and esteems itself but lightly in the flower of hope, before the fruits of the Spirit.

173. Once the habitation is prepared, it requires an inhabitant; the empty couch calls for a consort of love; enduring faith needs the gladness of one who enjoys God and delights in him. This is what the Bride says: "My Beloved belongs to me, and I to him." He belongs to me, she says, God making me for this very thing;[12] I belong to him, for I was made in order to belong to him. He belongs to me by conferring the advance gift of grace, and I to him by casting away ingratitude; he belongs to me by bestowing faith, and I to him by keeping it. And in the Bride's inner self, while she knows it not, the Bridegroom feeds upon what causes her torment, when she accepts no consolation apart from the embrace and the kiss and the sweetness of mutual union. Hence she goes on to say: "He feeds among the lilies."

174. The lily is the most beautiful of flowers, but sterile. Rising

12. Cf. 2 Cor 5:5.

from earth toward heaven on a straight green stalk, it is white without but flame-colored within; charming to the sight, sweet to the smell, possessing the natural virtue of softening things that are hard. Look at the lily before sunrise; as if taking refuge from the visage of nocturnal cold and the darkness of night, and hiding within itself, it closes up its fragile delights and keeps them for its own; but as soon as the face of the rising sun shines upon it from fair skies, you may see it open completely, as if smiling, and restore all its glory to its Creator.

This is exactly the state of the soul that has been rendered good by creative grace but still remains sterile as far as the fruits of understanding and wisdom are concerned; it awaits them from illuminating grace. This is the conscience whose will and intention are directed towards God, showing before men the whiteness of chastity and the outer works of faith, and before God the inner perfume of unceasing desire. It bears about the fragrance of Christ in every place, amid tribulations and anguish; it possesses the virtue of patience to soften all the hardness of human malice; and it keeps all its good things in the secret of creative God-given grace, until its justice is brought forth as the light and its judgment as the noonday in the clarity of illuminating grace.[13]

175. Now in the verb used in the line: "He feeds among the lilies," two persons are implied: he who feeds another, and he who is fed. The Bridegroom, then, feeds among the lilies (that is, he is fed) when this lily, the Bride, afflicted in conscience by her sterility, habitually delights him by the fruitfulness of her will. And he in turn feeds the Bride, although she is not aware of it, when in that very delaying he nourishes her love of him. Indeed the Bride well knows what is taking place in her, what the Bridegroom is accomplishing in her, inasmuch as they belong mutually one to the other; but she does not feel it, inasmuch as they are not mutually present one to the other. For they belong one to the other by faith, and they

13. Cf. Ps 36:6.

are present by love; or if you will, they belong one to the other by love, and they are present by affection. And all is well as long as they belong one to the other; but incomparably better when they are present one to the other. This is the meaning of what follows: "Till the day break and the shadows retire."

176. For when the day breaks and the shadows retire, Bridegroom and Bride will pass beyond the point of belonging one to the other for mutual accord and be present one to the other for their mutual enjoyment and delight. And the Bridegroom will no longer feed amid the sterile loveliness of the lilies, but amid the full fertility of the fruits of the Spirit. For when by the daybreak of the Holy Spirit our night in this life shall be light as the day,[14] for a moment, for an hour, and the shadows of worldly vanities shall retire, yielding to the light of truth—or rather in the sunset of this life, which is night and not light, and in the morning of the opening of the other life, and above all in the morning of eternity, on the day of the general resurrection, then Bridegroom and Bride will begin no longer to belong one to the other by faith, but to be mutually present by vision, face to face;[15] and the Bridegroom will not feed the Bride as it were among the sterile lilies in the flower of hope, but in the fruit of reality. And then all the shadows of the vanity of this world shall retire; that is, they shall be cast down from the pedestal of their self-esteem.

Then just as in the past the new sacraments of grace put an end to the old sacraments, so the Reality which is veiled by all the sacraments will utterly put an end to all sacraments. In the sacraments of the New Testament, it is true, the day of new grace began to break; but in that end of perfect consummation will come the full noonday when glass and riddle and that which is in part shall be done away, but there shall be the vision face to face and the plenitude of the highest Good.[16] The object which reason was accustomed to seek out, the understanding will now fix; what love burned to attain

14. Cf. Ps 138:12.   15. Cf. 1 Cor 13:12.   16. *Ibid.*

affection will now enjoy and delight in: understanding not of reason, but of illuminated love; affection in no way worked up by the one who feels it, but made in a divine manner by God, as the Apostle says: "He that makes us for this very thing is God."[17] All the moral force, the virtues, wills, intentions and affections of the man glorified with God, which are delivered through the power of the resurrection from the servitude of corruption and subjection to vanity,[18] will be immutably stabilized in full vision of what he had believed in an incomplete manner; in secure possession of what he had hoped for with trepidation; and in entire fruition of what he had loved by faith.

177. The day which breaks in this present life is changeable and does not possess continually the joy of its light; yet it does possess its hours, the comings and goings of that grace which shines upon the soul who comes to God to be enlightened. But the day of heaven, the day of eternity, the day added to days,[19] utterly disengaged from all the shadows of this world, is wholly given over to its light and its joy, without desire to want more, without fear of losing, without sorrow over loss. But in the meantime the expectation of the creature waiting for the revelation of the sons of God, groans and travails in pain even until now; and they who have the first fruits of the Spirit groan within themselves, waiting for the adoption of the sons of God, the redemption of their body.[20]

178. Grant, O Bridegroom of charity and chastity, that they who possess these first fruits may keep them; and on those who possess them not, deign to bestow them. So may your Bride, whoever she may be, the faithful soul languishing for you and fainting away, fainting after your salvation,[21] not for want of your salvation, have sometimes a foretaste here on earth of some of the hours of your day, until she receives the full day. Like faithful Abraham she rejoices in the sole thought of seeing your day, that she may see it

17. 2 Cor 5:5.   18. Cf. Rom 8:20.   19. Cf. Ps 60:7.
20. Cf. Rom 8:22f.   21. Cf. Ps 118:81.

and be glad,[22] and her joy no one may take from her.[23] O Day of days, O Day of strength, O Day added to days,[24] break upon those who, from the depths of the gloom of this world's night, hope in you and sigh and aspire to you, O Day who are and fail not, who remain unchanged while, within yourself, you change all things.

Already, from the first glow of your light which you, O Sun of justice, have breathed upon us, from the rays of your most dazzling truth, these shadows of death, the shadows of the vanity of this world, have somewhat declined for us, and the vanity of vanities[25] has become manifest to us, and it has become manifest and clearer than light to us that all things are vanity. And would that your truth might shine forth for us in itself to the same extent as, in its light, this vanity is apparent to us! To the prudent observer and to him who judges these things in the light of your truth, the fact that they are vain and contemptible is disclosed by their insurmountable indigence, innate misery and invariable failure. Therefore all the sons of your light,[26] and all who do not rebel against your light, give thanks to you, for you have so far enlightened them that in you all these vanities have now become clear and deceive them not. At times, it is true, these things still attract and hamper them; but they no longer love them with fondness, even though they are sometimes obliged to attend to them. For even if the memory of the world sometimes steals into the mind unawares, or comes to be thought of with a certain pleasure, the will immediately opposes it, as reason keeps watch over the memory. The Holy Spirit helps human weakness[27] and straightway, as your light breaks, those shadows decline through the contemplation of this vanity; and by the conception of your truth the will is so far turned toward your love that now it receives no pleasure outside of you. And your light, O Day of days, immediately strikes the soul with a horror of

22. Cf. Jn 8:56.

23. Cf. Jn 16:22.

24. Cf. Ps 60:7.

25. Cf. Eccles 1:2.

26. Cf. Jn 12:36.

27. Cf. Rom 8:26.

the memory of the world and, in place of the vain sweetness of worldly pleasure, bestows upon it a true and most bitter bitterness.

Forthwith, O Charity of the chaste generation[28] and Bridegroom of holy souls, in the time of these vicissitudes your Bride always devoted to you in will, sometimes crucified with desire and sometimes enjoying and delighting in love, and always crucified with desire as long as she cannot enjoy the delights of love, is powerless to obtain from you the stability in you of eternal joy. For even though she possesses this stability in the firm disposition of her good will (from the uprightness of her conscience in the continual desire of you), she does not possess it in affection. And since, according to the plan of your wisdom, the wish of your good pleasure and the judgment of your justice, you go and come, sometimes like a most agreeable hind and a most agreeable fawn you permit yourself to be caught by faith; often you deign to be held by meditation, and sometimes even to be caressed by love. But when you are held with greater passion and possessed with more intense delight, suddenly you slip away; and you take pleasure in the lovelorn anxiety and fatigue of her who pursues you, while she weeps and calls after you: "Return!"

28. Cf. Wis 4:1.

N

STANZA 5

Return, my Beloved! Be like a roe
Or a young hart upon the mountains of Bethel![1]

THESE WORDS of the Bride may be taken thus: If as long
as there is time succeeding time you grant not that I may
possess you forever, to enjoy you and delight in you, at
least be more speedy to return, just as you are swift to depart and
abandon me. O that your comings and goings might be more frequent, your flight longer deferred, your return swifter and your
presence more familiar and more lasting! Precious to me is your
presence, even though momentary; precious is access to you, even
though slight; the sight of you, even though it be but a glimpse by
the mind's eye; a faint murmur of your voice; a taste, though slight,
of your sweetness; the fragrance of your perfumes; the gracious
bestowal, even in smallest measure, of your kiss and your embraces.
For me all these things are the pledge of the Spirit,[2] the earnest of
eternal beatitude, the support of faith, the strength of hope, the
incentive of love. Return therefore, the Bride says, return. Return
even if you will straightway depart again. Gladden me by your
appearance; sadden me by your disappearance. Whatever comes to
me from you seems good to me, for you are good and do all things
well; and whether you depart or return, this affection ever consoles
me, however often I suffer absence on your part.

1. Song 2:17.   2. Cf. 2 Cor 1:22; 5:5.

180. And indeed, as we have already said above, by analogy with what takes place in fleshly love, we perceive a certain sense of experience as regards spiritual love and the affection of Bridegroom and Bride. Often the Bridegroom seems to play the game of wanton love with the Bride; repeatedly he snatches himself away from her love with violence and then restores himself again to her desires. Sometimes he withdraws and departs as if he would not return, to make her seek him with greater ardor; and sometimes he returns and comes where she is, as if he would remain forever, the more sweetly to invite her to receive his kisses. Sometimes he stands behind the wall and looks through the windows, to arouse his lover's desire by letting himself be seen with his charms, but not wholly, and letting his calls and invitations be heard, but from a distance. But once the fire, so to speak, is enkindled in the heart of his lover, he departs and withdraws, and is seen, heard and felt no more. The Bride is unable to stop him as he departs; but she entreats him at least to return from time to time and says: "Return, my Beloved: be like a roe or a young hart upon the mountains of Bethel!"

181. Blessed is the soul of the Bride, for she continually appeals to the Bridegroom by this name: "My Beloved!" For this is what Peter said: "Lord, you know that I love you!"[3] For when the beloved calls the Beloved by the name of Beloved, the name "Beloved" manifests and arouses her love, serves as her own commendation and attracts him whom she calls with her soul's devotion and love. Happy and auspiciously offered is prayer that in the Holy Spirit calls by this name the God to whom it prays! Blessed is the soul whose prayer is recommended by such inner confidence! If she prays thus, what may she not hope for? She prays that he whom she possesses may return—for she possesses him whom she loves. This is why Scripture says: "The Lord is nigh unto all them that call upon him in truth."[4] For in the affection of

3. Jn 21:15ff.   4. Ps 144:18.

the lover, the truth of her prayer becomes in her conscience, while
she prays, the firm proof of the most immediate presence of him
who said: "I am the truth."[5]

182. The Bride says therefore: "Return, my Beloved!" When
you are gone, all is trouble. When you turn away your face, holy
affections collapse in failure;[6] bitterness and unreasonable sadness
spring up in the conscience. In life with the brethren, scandals are
everywhere; in solitude, the mind is in tumult; inner light vanishes;
darkness envelops and crushes the soul. Faith languishes, hope
flickers, charity grows weary; the soul, become drunken, loses
control of itself; the body weighs down the spirit, and the spirit
the body. Prayer falters, reading is at a standstill, meditation is dry;
hardness of heart culminates in utter sterility of spirit, and the whole
world takes up arms against this foolish wretch.

But when you return, when you turn your face to me again, at
the gladness of your countenance, at the sweetness of perceiving
you, all is serenity and tranquillity. Holy happiness springs up in the
conscience; the understanding is lively, zeal is fervent, love is
enlightened, the spirit grows merry in God. The world seems
worthless; the body is a servant; the powers increase, the virtues
gain vigor. Faith is enlightened, hope is strengthened, and charity
is set in order; joy in the Holy Spirit is ever present. Life with the
brethren is sweet, and solitude with God still sweeter; the soul is
stable and rich in the spiritual senses. Prayer is swift, reading
profitable, meditation the fruit of reason, and spiritual effort brings
all to a happy issue. Activity takes on seriousness, and leisure is
sanctified; scandal and contradiction are met with no longer.
Success calls forth humility; misfortune, fortitude. As long as you,
armed in your strength, keep your court, all things you possess are
in peace.[7]

183. "Return," then, "my Beloved: be like a roe or a young
hart." What shall we say of the roe? It has very sharp sight. I have

---

5. Jn 14:6.   6. Cf. Ps 103:29.   7. Cf. Lk 11:21.

no wish, says the Bride, to be like Adam and hide myself from the face of him who, with approval or censure, sees all things.[8] Nay rather, I seek your countenance, O Lord; my face seeks your face.[9] For you will give keenness to my interior eyes, that I may contemplate you and give attention to myself. And as the hart is swift, you will give me swiftness of spirit to understand with regard to you, as your word runs swiftly.[10] And what shall we say about the young hart? It possesses the natural and hereditary property of putting serpents to flight and remaining unharmed by their venom. And thus wherever the Son of God turns, the old serpent is put to flight, and all his venom loses its power.

184. "Upon the mountains of Bethel": or "of Bether." Bethel means "house of God"; Bether, "house that rises up" or "house of vigils." Bethel therefore means those souls in whom God dwells with great familiarity, the sons of God, guileless, humble and peaceable; they fear his word, and the Holy Spirit rests upon them. It is the "house that rises up," always reaching up toward the heights; the "house of vigils" where watch is ever kept by those who, with devout and eager expectation, wait for the Bridegroom, the Lord, when he shall return from the wedding.[11]

185. The Bride therefore beseeches the Bridegroom to dwell more frequently over the house of Bethel or Bether, asking him to enlighten it in contemplation of him and to raise it up in contempt of the world for the love of God. And for the souls who keep their gaze fixed on him, she entreats him to acquaint them with the silent, interior joys of a good conscience in enjoyment of him. She also beseeches him to come more often upon the mountains, that is, upon the summit of human perfection, in order that the mountains may melt before the face of the Lord[12]—that is, that men, however great they may be, should account themselves as nothing in comparison with God, nothing without his grace.

8. Cf. Gen 3:8.
10. Cf. Ps 147:15.
9. Cf. Ps 26:8. See above, note 17, p. 28.
11. Cf. Lk 12:36.   12. Cf. Ps 96:5.

186. Thus the Bride of Christ, the faithful soul, is sometimes allowed in a certain measure to contemplate her joy, unable though she is to stop very long to delight in it. But this favor, whatever it is, sometimes falls to one who expects it not and again suddenly escapes one who possesses it; and this bears out what follows: "Be like the roe or a young hart." Here the word which is used—"be"—expresses the agreement of man's will with the will of God, when this human will is well disposed and firmly established in faith; for whether he deigns to visit the suppliant or appears to withdraw and forsake him, whatever, in his supreme goodness, God may do is good for the soul concerned. When he visited her, she possessed him with delight; and the moment he escapes her, she anxiously seeks him; this bears out what follows: "In my bed by night I sought him whom my soul loves."

STANZA 6

In my little bed by night
I sought him whom my soul loves:
I sought him and found him not.
I will rise and will go about the city;
In the streets and in the broad ways
I will seek him whom my soul loves.[1]

HERE we must first remark that when day vanishes, it is night; and in the absence of light, the eyes of the body open vainly in the darkness. In like manner, without the help of illuminating grace, the Bride strives in vain, by the power of reason and will, to contemplate the object of her desire. This is why she says: "In my little bed by night I sought him whom my soul loves." But first we must see what this passage signifies for us according to the letter.[2] The Bride in quest of the Bridegroom can have no leisure either by day or by night. For according to the letter, souls who are given to watching know how much opportunity night vigils afford for the pursuit of spiritual exercises, and what fruits of the Spirit they impart to those who keep watch for the Bridegroom's return. This is surely the special hour of the soul and of the things of the soul. The senses are inactive and make no trouble.

1. Song 3:1f.
2. This reminds us of St Bernard who in his *Sermons on the Song of Songs* frequently considers the literal sense before passing on to the spiritual sense; see e.g. Sermons 42, 51, 56, 58, 59, etc.

First comes the solitude of the place of rest; then, through sleep, repose for the body when, after the daily labors and troubles of this life, he who meditates on God is comforted, like holy Job, on his bed.[3] His bed is not the tomb of a dead man or a tavern of drunkenness, but a workshop of spiritual endeavors and a place of sacred visions, where it is sweet to dream what it was sweet to think of, and where what was not made known during the vigil is often revealed during sleep. Then once the viands, cares and anxieties of the preceding day have been digested, sobriety reigns again in soul and body. A fasting stomach more effectively consumes the viands it first receives, digests them more agreeably and assimilates them better; in the same way, for one who awakens, his fasting spirit lays firm hold on the first thought it meets with and retains it, especially in the case of one it finds congenial. That is why when she who is a Bride wakens after sober slumber, sufficient only for the bare needs of nature,[4] she must chiefly preoccupy herself with being straightway united to the Bridegroom, as a virgin and hitherto unstained, adhering to God, and being entirely drawn to him, insofar as she may. The result of this will be that henceforth, remaining the entire day and entire night holy and without blemish, in both body and spirit, she is not divided but belongs entirely to him who finds her pleasing;[5] she accepts no admixture of any other base affection.

188. Now to take this in a more profound sense, the Bride lost the Bridegroom out of doors, yet she seeks him within, in the bed of her heart, in the solitude of her spirit, in her conscience. Out of doors the action of the drama takes place: the Bridegroom commands, and the Bride obeys. But within, the business of love, secret colloquies and hidden mysteries are transacted, at least while the Bridegroom is still present. For when the Bridegroom is absent,

3. Cf. Job 7:13.

4. William treats more at length of sleep and its benefits when taken in due proportion in his *Letter to the Carthusians of Mont Dieu*, nos. 135ff.

5. Cf. 1 Cor 7:33f.

there is unending night, fearful solitude, tiresome waiting, no rest whatever. Although he is always there by his unfailing power, nevertheless, by a secret design of his wisdom, he is not continually there by his directing grace. For as Solomon says: "There is a time to embrace and a time to be far from embrace."[6] This is why she adds these words: "I sought him and found him not."

189. When she finds him not, she calls him with a loud cry because of the great desire with which she pants for him; but he makes no answer to her call, as long as he does not grant access to himself according to her prayers and desires. She carries on her search by night; it is not irksome to her to pass many a night in the quest. The darkness of this life, the profound gloom of the world and the night of temptations and tribulations, even though they sometimes hamper her, are unable to stop her zealous pursuit. Blessed is the man that fears all his works[7] and is always fearful [8]— not as wickedness is ever wont to be timid, but as human blindness and weakness ought invariably to mistrust themselves. Only she who loves, and she who is a Bride, knows these tribulations of love regarding the Bridegroom, the torment of hope deferred, the joy of possessing him, the fear of losing him, the grief of having lost him. She could not do better than seek him in her bed, for she constantly strives to have him with her on her couch, making ready for him the bed of her heart, that she may possess him in her conscience and in meditation, in understanding and love and in the service of her devotion, joined to the testimony of the deeds she devotes to him.

190. "I sought him" therefore, she says, "in my little bed," where I have been wont to find him more familiarly and more frequently. I sought, and I sought in truth to know whether he was there, so that by progress in the order of charity I might also be present, in the joy of vision and the sweetness of enjoyment and delight, with him who is ever wont to be nigh unto all them that call upon him

6. Eccles 3:5.   7. Cf. Job 9:28.   8. Cf. Prov 28:14.

in truth.[9] "I sought him and I found him not." Why was this? Perchance because it was night; and it may well have happened that once her purpose grew weary, light for her search, together with fervor and warmth of desire, somewhat diminished. For if she had sought him through love, she would have found him in understanding; and she would have been supremely happy in his embrace.

191. But this seems a more suitable interpretation:[10] The Bridegroom approaches the Bride in order to comfort her weariness, and he may sometimes withdraw in order to confirm or even to kindle her desire for him. For desires that die out because of deferment are not desires at all. This is why the Bride discloses what her course of action will be in the Bridegroom's absence, when she goes on to say: "I will rise and go about the city; in the streets and in the broad ways I will seek him whom my soul loves."

192. What city is this? What streets and broad ways are these, in which it seems the Bridegroom must be sought and yet is not found? No doubt it is the city of which the Psalm says: "I have seen iniquity and contradiction in the city. Day and night shall iniquity surround it upon its walls; and in the midst thereof are labor and injustice. And usury and deceit have not departed from its streets."[11] There the man of one mind, who did take sweet meats together with the Bridegroom himself, has greatly supplanted him.[12] There the flesh lusts against the spirit[13] and neighbor against neighbor.

193. What city is this? The world. What city is this? I say it with sorrow: the profane world and the Church in the world. I will say more, and I will say it with grief: every religious order, of whatever habit. If the world, which is of the world, busies itself with the things of the world, we suffer it more patiently and lament less

---

9. Cf. Ps 144:18.

10. Unlike St Bernard who is accustomed to offer various interpretations for a single text (see *supra*, Stanza 1, note 12), it is unusual for William to offer an alternate interpretation.

11. Ps 54:10ff.   12. Cf. Ps 54:14f.; 40:10.   13. Cf. Gal 5:17.

about it; this is because we are used to it and have no hope that things will be otherwise. But in the Church of the living God, which, as the Apostle says, is the pillar and ground of the truth,[14] above all in the religious orders which make profession of zeal for a stricter life, who would not weep, yes, weep tears of blood, tears from his heart, that those dangerous times have come which the Apostle foresaw in the last days, when men would be lovers of themselves, having an appearance indeed of godliness but denying the power thereof?[15]

194. At present, this city is the whole world. And if in some respects it seems to be Jerusalem, rightfully and without any contradiction do Syria and Damascus reduce it for their own use to a military post and broad ways.[16] For who is there today professing the poverty of Christ that does not labor and strive to burst his pockets with money and stuff his purse until he more than rivals the rich of this world? The larger portion of the world is the property of religious men! In the wilderness, palaces are being erected; in deserts and caves, perfumed cells are built.[17] No one who

---

14. Cf.1 Tim 3:15.   15. Cf. 2 Tim 3:1ff.   16. Cf. 1 Kings 20:34.

17. Poverty for William was an important element of monastic life. In his earlier work, *On the Nature and Dignity of Love*, when he described the ideal monastic community, poverty and simplicity had a prominent place (trans. Webb and Walker, ch. 8, p. 39). In his final work, his *Letter to the Carthusians of Mont Dieu*, inspite of his enthusiastic admiration of them he did not hesitate to speak strongly, in terms reminiscent of this section of the *Exposition*, of their lack of true poverty and simplicity (nos. 147ff.). In this he was identifying with the spirit of the founders of Cîteaux, as is evident from chs. 15 and 17 of the *Little Exordium*. It is well known what emphasis Bernard of Clairvaux placed in his *Apologia to Abbot William* (trans. M. Casey, "Cistercians and Cluniacs" in *The Works of Bernard of Clairvaux,* vol. 1 [Cistercian Fathers Series 1], nos. 16ff.). St Bernard expresses his deep conviction very succinctly in his Fourth Sermon for Advent, no. 5: "A powerful wing is evangelical poverty, which enables us to fly speedily to the kingdom of heaven. Observe that the other virtues which follow in the beatitudes obtain only a promise of this kingdom, to be fulfilled at a future time; but to poverty it is not so much promised as actually given."—trans. B. Saïd, in *The Works of Bernard of Clairvaux,* vol. 4 (Cistercian Fathers Series 10).

enters religion will condescend to make the shortest of journeys on his own feet. Monks rejoice to be called Christians or disciples of Christ, but in this matter their imitation of the example of Christ and that of Christ's disciples is, to put it very mildly, insufficient. Has a monk never ridden a horse? Then he must learn; and if he knows how to ride, he blushes to unlearn the art. What corner is to be found today where there are not many instances of that sin so much insisted on by the Apostle, namely that we have lawsuits one with another?[18] And would that these lawsuits, as their name [*judicia*] implies, might be just and not unjust! I grant that we do not rob or cheat; but although we are not robbers or cheaters, we can consent not to make the most of our time; thus we protect ourselves against losing anything, or working and eating our own bread in silence.[19] Through concupiscence for the world we become submissive to men of the world, fawning on sinners while we seek not them but their goods. Are not these the broad ways of the world by which we travel toward death? Are not these the streets of the world, different to be sure, yet resembling the way of life of the world? If we were really wise, we would fear the words spoken by that chosen vessel, the Apostle Paul,[20] concerning men that have nothing yet possess all things:[21] "Those who seek to become rich fall into temptations and the snares of the devil and into many and harmful desires, which plunge men into the destruction of damnation."[22] For on every occasion and under every pretext, covetousness, which is always the root of all evils, creeps in; and they who are eager to get rich involve themselves in many troubles.[23]

But nonetheless, amid such a great company of rich men that laugh at the danger to which they are exposed, one is sometimes found who is poor in spirit, a man of God, to whom, as if snatched

18. Cf. 1 Cor 6:7.
20. Cf. Acts 9:15.
22. 1 Tim 6:9.

19. Cf. 2 Thess 3:12.
21. Cf. 2 Cor 6:10.
23. Cf. 1 Tim 6:10.

from the whirlpool of a stormy sea and brought with him to the harbor of most calm and peaceful charity, the same Apostle would say: "But you, O man of God, flee these things; but pursue justice, godliness, faith, charity, patience, mildness. Fight the good fight of faith, lay hold on the life eternal."[24] Whoever is a man of God flees and escapes the vices we have been referring to, laboring with all his might but casting off all his anxiety upon God.[25] He avoids carelessness and places his confidence in God, always keeping a firm desire to please him. He has the good will to agree with all men and to covet without sin, obtaining whatever he can by labor and administering whatever he has obtained with prudence and liberality. Everywhere he calls forth and seeks affection and love; he execrates and shuns the desire to please. For a religious order ruled by covetousness differs in no wise from the broad ways of Syria and Damascus in Jerusalem;[26] and those are streets wherein the Bridegroom is not found.

195. "In the streets and in the broad ways I sought him whom my soul loves." How is this? Surely the Bridegroom is not in a public place? In the broad ways and streets? But impatient love imagines that he must be sought everywhere, and that nowhere can he fail to be found when he wishes to be found.

196. The Bride says, "him whom my soul loves." Why does she not rather say, "him whom my spirit loves"? Because it is not the spiritual that comes first but the animal, and then the spiritual.[27] By the soul which vivifies, we are to understand life; this is the figure of speech which names the effect by its cause. We see that the Bride's soul loves and seeks the Bridegroom inasmuch as for her to live is Christ,[28] Christ is glorified in her life, she profits by everything that is and lives in him, and she desires to live only that every living being may be subject to him.

197. And so, she says, "I sought him whom my soul loves." In her sorrow at the flight of him she was holding, she goes about

24. Cf. 1 Tim 6:11f.   25. Cf. 1 Pet 5:7.   26. Cf. 1 Kings 20:34.
27. Cf. 1 Cor 15:46.   28. Cf. Phil 1:21.

everywhere, making the rounds of every place, every occupation, every kind of man, every way of life. She feels only disgust for beautiful sights, savory smells, harmonious sounds, fragrant perfumes, caressing contacts, desirable possessions, radiant delights. The stability of love makes her unstable; the firm purpose of her will makes her fickle; the unchangeableness of her love makes her changeable. She is eager to seek him wherever there is a hope he may be found, although he is wont sometimes to be found even where there is no such hope. But she finds some trace of the Bridegroom everywhere and in every person in whom she finds any token of virtue, any example of devotion, any reflection of innocence, any flame of religion, any love of purity.

"Him whom my soul loves." Blessed again and again, and ever blessed, is the soul of her who says to the Lord her God, unceasingly in her conscience and often with her lips: "him whom my soul loves!"

I sought him, and I found him not.
The watchmen who keep the city found me.
Have you seen him whom my soul loves?

When I had a little passed by them,
I found him whom my soul loves.[1]

L ET US go back a little over what we have already said in
order to consider the historical sense and the plan of the
drama. The Bridegroom came to the Bride, leaping upon the
mountains and skipping over the hills. Looking through the windows and peering through the lattices, he saw her inactive in the idle
busyness or busy idleness of her little bed, all her actions and
thoughts bent upon this. Once, twice, thrice he summoned her to
arise, make haste and come; he invited her to the more hidden
mysteries of his love, to the beholding of a more perfect vision of
him, to the consideration of a clearer knowledge of him, to the more
exalted gifts of eternal beatitude. But after this he departed, withdrew into the secret of his divinity and hid from her his face, that
longed-for face on which not only the angels in heaven but men on
earth, rivals of angelic perfection, desire to gaze.[2] He made darkness
his covert.[3]

Since the Bride had been cherished with greater tenderness and
brought up in the delights of grace, the undeserved visits of the

1. Song 3:2ff.   2. Cf. 1 Pet 1:12.   3. Cf. Ps 17:12.

Bridegroom made her the more slothful; neglecting spiritual exercises, she gave herself wholly to prayer, spiritual leisure and meditation, with no care for anything else. This is why, when the Bridegroom called her, she did not arise, did not make haste and did not come; instead, she entreated him to return to her more frequently, saying: "Return! Be like a roe or a young hart!" And when he does not return in answer to her prayers and entreaties, she turns from side to side as if she were unable to extend her foot from the delights and warmth of her little bed. She seeks in her bed, but without the labor of spiritual exercises, the kisses and embraces to which she is accustomed; and she always trusts that she will find there, but without the weariness of outward labor, the grace of her accustomed delight.

But since the Bridegroom tarries, she finally perceives that she must arise, realizing that it would be more fitting for her to come forth at the Bridegroom's command than to remain alone, or rather to indulge her sloth, in the little bed of her idleness in the Bridegroom's absence. Finally she comes to the conclusion that idleness without him is not rest but more like being buried alive. And so she says: "I will arise and will go about the city. In the streets and in the broad ways I will seek him whom my soul loves." This amounts to saying: I will go out and seek an opportunity for a good deed as a help to my interior contemplation.[4] "I will seek," she says, "him whom my soul loves." The more authentic manuscripts read thus: *him,* she says, *whom she loves.*

199. For it now seems to the Bride as if she loves not the Bridegroom so long as the flame of his divine goodness fails to kindle her affection for him—so long as the remembrance of the wealth of his sweetness fails to attract her memory and inform her understanding. When the Bridegroom departs, all the Bride's consolations suddenly vanish and take to flight. Her soul is rendered barren of its former fruits. Her love is empty of attraction, her thought devoid

---

4. St Bernard too advises the monk when the consolations of contemplation are withdrawn to turn to good works. Cf. Sermon 51 on the Song of Songs.

of understanding and the fruit of devotion. I will arise, therefore, she says. I will go wherever the ferment of my love, or rather of my desire, impels me. I will follow wherever it leads me. And in the meantime, since I am unworthy that the Bridegroom should visit me with the accustomed grace, I will seek men whom God has formed for this very purpose, that by enjoying them in God, I may enjoy God in them. For they are sometimes to be found in the broad ways, since, alas! they are not to be found in cloisters; they are to be found in the streets, since they are not to be found in hermitages. Not that they are not more often in cloisters and more familiarly in hermitages, but when a person seeks God, he is never to be found unless he himself first finds the one who is seeking him; and likewise he never fails to be found when he anticipates the one who is seeking him.

200. "The watchmen who keep the city found me." Watchmen we understand to mean either ministering angels, sent for the service of those who enter into the inheritance of salvation, or holy doctors and preachers, appointed to guard the city of the Church, each of them in their watch stations. For there are angels of God's poor and of his little ones, who ever behold the face of the Lord;[5] according to the judgment of his countenance, they help and protect her who is a Bride, giving her useful advice and salutary counsels through certain secret forms of suggestion. The Bride tells the Bridegroom that she questioned these watchmen, but she does not say they gave her any answer. Divine answers, whether given by secret inspiration, angelic ministry or human teaching, are not always at hand for all our questions, especially in the hour of temptation.

201. There are also holy doctors of the Church—shepherds watching and keeping the night watches over their flock,[6] through whom, either by the words of those still living on earth or by the writings of those now reigning with God, a divine answer is always

5. Cf. Mt 18:10. 6. Cf. Lk 2:8.

at hand for us in the hour of prosperity and illuminating grace, often replying to our secrets and our needs. But, in the hour of tribulation, in the days of captivity, the heavens become brass and the ground iron.[7] There is neither prophet nor prophecy, no vision from the Lord;[8] the word perishes from the doctor, and counsel from the wise.[9] By word, writing or example, these watchmen find the Bride in her search but fail to help her. Hers is the usual lot of the wretched. She has many counselors, but not one helper, for when God turns away his face, all is trouble.[10] Words remain nothing but words, and writings nothing but letters. A crowd of people shout in her ears, but no one speaks to her sorrowful heart. No one replies to her questions; no one puts out a hand to guide her into the right path.

202. "The watchmen who keep the city found me." Grace had not yet made her loving, yet they found her seeking. But they could not have found her there if prevenient grace had not been given her. Just as none of the senses can be made understandable to one who lacks it (for instance, sight to one who has never seen, or hearing to him who has never heard, and so on), so neither, or rather so much the less, can the interior sense of grace be given to him who does not possess it or restored to him who has lost it. They who possess the joy of the Lord may preach it and commend it to those who do not possess it. They may advise them how to seek it and tell them a way to recover it; and sometimes even, if grace is present, the will may be moved and desire excited. But this joy is tasted only by him into whom it pours itself. No one ascends this summit unless it bends down to him; no one feels this good unless it conforms him to itself; no one lives by this life unless it imparts itself to him.

203. The watchmen therefore have been passed by. As they could not induce the Bride to seek him, neither could they make her successful in finding him. In a word, charity is poured forth in our

7. Cf. Deut 28:23.   8. Cf. 1 Sam 3:1.
9. Cf. Jer 18:18.   10. Cf. Ps 103:29.

hearts not by the teaching of man but by the Holy Spirit who is given to us.[11] And no word, whatever its source, is effective unless the power of prevenient grace is operative in it. This is why she says to the watchmen: "Have you seen him whom my soul loves?"

Here are two things, she says, that do not sound alike. The sound of the inner sweetness of my soul does not say the same thing to me as the outward word of your preaching. My love has a certain sense of him whom I seek, and you experience it likewise; but your words do not express it, nor do those of any man. You experience it far better and more deservedly than I, but through your words, nevertheless, we do not find the object of our search, and neither do you attain what you desire. In fine you have much to say to us, but you do not win us over, because you have not learned to know the Reality as it is. The consolations derived from reading your works and the spiritual meditations they occasioned have been very useful to us, and we must say the same of the assiduous prayers and other spiritual or corporal exercises we have performed in imitation of your holy desire; but nevertheless you must be passed by in all these matters.

For we must finally accomplish our journey where we shall no longer read except in the Book of Truth; where Eternal Wisdom shall be given instead of meditation; vision, instead of consolation; the face to face, instead of the glass and the riddle.[12] But this is far beyond you, since it is the state of the future life and eternal beatitude, which exceeds and transcends all weakness. But only a little beyond you is the state of devotion in which the Bridegroom sometimes helps the weakness of his Bride, whoever she is, that she may gain a foretaste of these things. The air beyond the moon, beneath the vault of heaven, is said to be free from rain, hail, winds and all tempests, abiding in perpetual calm. In like manner the state of the good soul, attained through progress in virtue, is freed from the lower darkness and illuminated at closer range by the splendor from above.

11. Cf. Rom 5:5.   12. Cf. 1 Cor 13:12.

ANALYTIC INDEX

Numbers refer to the paragraphs of the text.

CISTERCIAN STUDIES SERIES

Under the direction of the same Board of Editors as the CISTERCIAN FATHERS SERIES, the CISTERCIAN STUDIES SERIES seeks to make available to the English-speaking world significant studies produced in other languages, as well as various monastic texts and studies of perennial value, with a view to placing the Cistercian Fathers in their full historical context and bringing out their present-day relevance.

CS1   Thomas Merton: *The Climate of Monastic Prayer*
Introduction: Douglas V. Steere

CS2   Amédée Hallier, *The Monastic Theology of Aelred o, Rievaulx: An Experiential Theology*
Introduction: Thomas Merton

CS3   *The Cistercian Spirit: A Symposium*
In Memory of Thomas Merton (Fr Louis ocso)

CS4   Evagrius Ponticus: *The Praktikos and 153 Chapters on Prayer*

Cistercian Publications   Spencer Massachusetts 01562

Irish University Press   Shannon   Ireland

171